The Free and the Virtuous

The Free and the Virtuous

Why the Founders Knew that Character Mattered

Heather Dutton Dudley

LEXINGTON BOOKS
Lanham • Boulder • New York • London

Published by Lexington Books
An imprint of The Rowman & Littlefield Publishing Group, Inc.
4501 Forbes Boulevard, Suite 200, Lanham, Maryland 20706
www.rowman.com

6 Tinworth Street, London SE11 5AL, United Kingdom

Copyright © 2020 by The Rowman & Littlefield Publishing Group, Inc.

All rights reserved. No part of this book may be reproduced in any form or by any electronic or mechanical means, including information storage and retrieval systems, without written permission from the publisher, except by a reviewer who may quote passages in a review.

British Library Cataloguing in Publication Information Available

Library of Congress Cataloging-in-Publication Data

Names: Dutton Dudley, Heather, 1955– author.
Title: The free and the virtuous : why the founders knew that
    character mattered / Heather Dutton Dudley.
Other titles: Why the founders knew that character mattered
Description: Lanham : Lexington Books, [2020] | Includes bibliographical
    references and index. | Summary: "For the American founding fathers,
    good character was not just important to the survival of liberty, it was
    the load bearing central pillar. Today this is no longer true. Good
    character doesn't matter. The author examines why and how this complete
    abandonment of the founders' value system came about"— Provided by
    publisher.
Identifiers: LCCN 2020030766 (print) | LCCN 2020030767 (ebook) | ISBN
    9781793601605 (cloth) | ISBN 9781793601612 (epub) | ISBN 9781793601629 (pbk)
Subjects: LCSH: Founding Fathers of the United States. | United
    States—Politics and government—1783–1809. | Character--Political
    Aspects—United States—History. | Social values—United
    States—History. | Political culture—United States—History. | Liberty.
Classification: LCC E302.1 .D83 2020 (print) | LCC E302.1 (ebook) | DDC
    973.3092/2—dc23
LC record available at https://lccn.loc.gov/2020030766
LC ebook record available at https://lccn.loc.gov/2020030767

Contents

Acknowledgments		vii
Introduction: Words about a Word		ix
1	The Four-Note Chord of Liberty	1
2	The American Creed	9
3	The Classical Roots of Virtue	19
4	Greek Eleutheria and Roman Liberatas	31
5	Two Paths to Virtue: Religion and Reason	39
6	Benjamin Franklin and Thomas Jefferson: The Art of Moderation	49
7	Virtue or Rights?	69
8	More Need of Masters	83
9	Liberty: The Box with the False Bottom	95
Conclusion: Mourning Virtue		107
Bibliography		115
Index		123
About the Author		125

Acknowledgments

I would like to thank all of my professors in the Doctor of Liberal Studies program at Georgetown University in Washington, DC. You changed the way I think. The study of human values was the area of overlap in my personal Venn diagram of academic interests: history and psychology. There were areas of scholarship where I knew a little; others where I knew a bit more. The valuable feedback from Ori Soltes and Charles Yonkers were particularly helpful with filling out the former, and helping to clarify the latter. Without a doubt, Thomas Kerch was the best mentor that I could have hoped for. He offered the perfect balance between reassurance and critique. He encouraged me to believe that I could write and helped to untangle my thoughts when I clearly could not.

I would like to acknowledge the patience and forbearance of my friends and family, and most especially my children, Thomas and Austin, for putting up with all of my spontaneous history lectures. I would never have finished this project without the encouragement from my husband. Thank you, Tim, for your unwavering and unconditional support through all my hand-wringing, head-thumping, and self-doubt. You were my eagle-eyed proofreader, and never questioned why I needed to complete this project.

Introduction

Words about a Word

Suffering from the accumulated maladies of old age and just two weeks before his death, eighty-three-year-old Thomas Jefferson wrote his last letter. It was a letter to regret an invitation. Poor health caused him to decline a request to attend a celebration of the fiftieth anniversary of the Declaration of Independence to be held in the city of Washington. As Jefferson would occasionally and wonderfully do in his letters, in this polite correspondence he veered into the loftiest reflections on the nature of human existence. The success of American independence had been about nothing less than "the fate of the world." Jefferson wrote that a signal had been heard around the world that would encourage the establishment of self-government, "to some parts sooner, to others later, but finally to all." The enjoyment of the "unbounded exercise of reason and freedom of opinion" had revealed "the palpable truth that the mass of mankind has not been born, with saddles on their backs, nor a favored few booted and spurred, ready to ride them.... Mankind had broken the chains of ignorance and superstition and had chosen to live free."[1]

Jefferson's letter—a valedictory address of sorts—was a reminder of what the founders' fight for independence had been all about. As historic as that certainly was, it had been so much more than a political event that concerned a colony breaking away from an empire. It had been about mankind taking a great leap forward in the progress of liberty. A new genus of liberty had taken root in the fresh soil of America. The purpose of this book is to rediscover that early understanding of American liberty. It was not just about limited government, protecting rights, and leaving people free to define their own lives. It was to be a movement toward the highest human flourishing. The founders of the Revolutionary generation believed that Americans were up to the task. They believed that a special something—a moral discipline—would be an enduring part of the make-up of the American people. Above all else, real liberty was dependent upon character. Unfortunately, Americans have lost sight of what liberty was originally all about.

As I will explain in the following chapters, the new nation had barely gotten any traction when the founders' ideal of a liberty based upon virtue began to lose its luster. Liberty gradually became more about rights and less about the responsibility to be good. As the pressure to sustain the hard work of virtuous living—and yes, it was hard!—the responsibility to create a happy life gradually shifted from it being the responsibility of each individual citizen to it being the concern of the national government.

Ideas have histories; and no idea has a more complex history than liberty. Hegel wrote that history is the history of liberty. If true, then the history of the United States is one of the most important chapters. Although this nation's history has been periodically marred by visceral attempts to assert that one ethnic, religious, or racial group was more American than another, to be an American does in fact mean that one belongs to a community that is unified by an idea: liberty to pursue the good life is an unalienable right. The United States was the first nation to be founded not upon myth, conquest, or accident—as most others have before—but upon a demand for the protection of that fundamental right.

The origins of the United States are not obscured by the vagaries of the ancient past. We do not reach back to a Herodotus-type history, where fact and fiction are blended to inform, entertain, and impress. The United States was founded in the bright light of recent history. We know who the founders were, what they wrote, who they read, and—as tenuous as it might be for one person to ever claim this about another—what they were thinking. We assemble the men who were instrumental in the formation of the United States and label the collective "the Founding Fathers." This singular term is unfortunate for they were a group that was riven by conflict, with the major players shifting positions in the critical years between the Declaration of Independence and the Constitution. A happy band of brothers they were not.

Jefferson wrote the Declaration but was absent from the Constitutional Convention and was an early critic of the document that the delegates produced. Leading supporters of independence such as Patrick Henry and Thomas Paine turned bitter critics of where they believed the newly independent nation was headed. *Federalist Papers* collaborators James Madison and Alexander Hamilton became political enemies with the rise of party politics. In the early period of the republic Jefferson was, according to John Adams's wife Abigail, "a respected Friend" and was "the only person with whom my Companion could associate; with perfect freedom, and unreserve."[2] A little over a decade later Jefferson referred to Adams' presidency as "the reign of witches" that he hoped would soon "pass over, their spells dissolve, and the people recovering their true sight, restore their government to it's true principles."[3] Yet despite their many differences, one supreme conviction unified them. This was their shared truth: the protection of liberty was the raison d'etre of good government. The United States was not just a country, it was a cause.

Liberty in America has always been the first principle of political and social life and the ultimate banner word upon which any cause hoping to gain traction will center its rhetoric. Jefferson proclaimed in 1780 that the soon to be independent nation would be the "Empire of Liberty"[4] and since that time the rhetoric of liberty has headlined every major issue in American history, from relations with Europe, western expansion, immigration, labor issues, and war. The need to defend and promote liberty at home and abroad has been the decisive cause mentioned before entering both world wars, and underpinned the West's cold war ideology. Nations that do not encourage liberty are simply thought of as wrong; or in recent decades, in need of rebuilding.

In 1823 the aging Jefferson, although claiming no longer to be interested in political subjects, wrote to President James Monroe concerning a topic that he considered to be "the most momentous which has ever been offered to my contemplation since that of independence." The issue—it was ultimately addressed in what was called the Monroe Doctrine—that stirred the octogenarian Jefferson from his retirement was the need "to make our hemisphere that of freedom" by protecting the newly independent South American nations from European interference.[5] The United States, however, should only spread its influence in the name of freedom. This ideology was captured in the phrase "manifest destiny," and construed westward national expansion as a religious mission to spread freedom; it justified the acquisition of Oregon and a war of conquest with Mexico.

Thirty years before the Civil War, Daniel Webster presciently stated what the northern cause would be: "Liberty and Union, now and forever, one and inseparable!" Webster's greatest contemporary and adversary, John C. Calhoun, knew as well that the great cause that would tear the nation apart was how to protect liberty. When Calhoun said "the Union, next to our liberty, most dear" he was affirming what the next generation of southern secessionists believed. If the Union did not protect their freedom to maintain and expand slavery then the Union could not be preserved. One great idea, and two magnificently opposed ways of framing it was the cause of the greatest American tragedy.

If it was the unique destiny of the American people to promote freedom, there must be some special quality in the American people that deserved protection. True, the New World promised freedom, but maybe not all the emigrants from the Old World were prepared to defend it. This fear that freedom could be undermined by immigrants who might not be able to understand American liberty has been at the heart of worries over immigration that have existed throughout American history. Our most well-known national symbol is the Statue of Liberty that welcomes immigrants "yearning to breathe free," but might some of the "wretched refuse" coming ashore be ultimately harmful to American freedom? As early as 1787 Jefferson expressed a concern that would reemerge throughout history, from the Alien and Sedition Acts of 1798, to the Chinese Exclusion Act of 1882, to the Immigration Restriction Act of 1921, to President Donald Trump's 2018 Muslim ban. Jefferson observed that our government was uniquely composed "of the freest principles," and would therefore attract the greatest number of immigrants. These immigrants, Jefferson feared, would "bring with them the principles of the government [mostly monarchical] they leave, imbibed in their early youth; or, if able to throw them off, it will be in exchange for an unbounded licentiousness. . . . It would be a miracle were they to stop precisely at the point of temperate liberty."[6]

Immigration restrictions framed as policies that would protect American liberty did not stretch the concept nearly as much as what happened when it came to the labor issue. During the rise of industrial capitalism in the late nineteenth century, individual liberty was expanded to include freedom from government regulation in the labor market. The *free* market meant no government interference. The invisible hand could only work the magic if left alone. In the 1905 case *Lochner v. New York*, the Supreme Court ruled that the "right to make a contract in relation to his business is part of the liberty of the individual protected by the Fourteenth Amendment of the Federal Constitution."[7] This case was so influential that the following three decades came to be known as the Lochner Era. Since "no State can deprive any person of life, liberty or property without due process of law" it followed that "the right to purchase or to sell labor is part of the liberty protected by this amendment."[8] Courts would strike down attempts by the state to improve conditions for workers, many of whom had no choice but to work one hundred-hour weeks in brutal conditions. The fourteenth amendment, passed to protect the rights of freed slaves, was interpreted in such a way that the often-brutal treatment of men, women, and children in the factories could continue. All for the sake of liberty.

These quick highlights from American history illuminate this point: liberty has been stretched to validate just about any policy. Many of these problems are no longer with us, the context shifts, but the underlying theme of liberty seems to connect all issues. One principle, however, certainly cannot be used to support all arguments. Along the way, we must have lost the clear conception of what we are talking about. The defense of liberty has become such a programmed part of the dialogue, and so worn out by overuse that we no longer wonder about what it really means.

The founders had a crystal-clear picture of what the ideal of liberty was all about. They knew what was involved and how it could be preserved or lost. "We mutually pledge to each other our Lives, our Fortunes and our sacred Honor," are the words that close the Declaration of Independence, and they are as important as any other line in that great document. Liberty was an idea they were willing to die for; and people do not die for vague jargon. There were four clear principles that were inextricably connected to the founders' idea of liberty. They were repeatedly written about in the voluminous writings of the day. They resonated with such power that the founders believed they were not just meant to apply to the specific events of their times but would take on universal applicability.

A metaphor of a four-note musical chord can help capture the way four principles were linked in such a way as to produce one state of mind. Each of the four components can be thought of as one note in a four-note musical chord. The four notes are: (1) personal liberty—the ability to do as one pleases within the rule of law, (2) political liberty—the right to participate in the government that makes those laws, (3) internal liberty—the ability to gain control over passions and destructive impulses that prevent a person from making good choices and passing good laws, and (4) public good liberty—a benevolent consciousness of, and participation in, the well being of the community. All four types of liberty were understood as necessarily working together. There was a stable harmony. No single idea rang louder than the others; nor were they ranked in order of importance. In the four-note chord of liberty, personal and internal liberty were balanced and a virtuous person would self-limit behavior that was harmful to the public good. Chapter 1 will delve a bit deeper into this novel approach to understanding liberty.

Chapter 2 will focus on the Declaration of Independence. The emphasis will be on how the document connected liberty to happiness and how happiness was really all about virtue. Today we honor the Declaration without realizing how profoundly this nation has disconnected from the original meaning of the words that the document celebrated. The National Archives can preserve the parchment, but the conceptual additions and subtractions from mental constructs can happen slowly and outside of awareness. This examination will serve as the first bridge from today, to the founders' generation, and to classical antiquity. Happiness is a goal that has not lost its importance over the years. Its original meaning most certainly has.

The word "happiness" in a recent search on Google resulted in over one hundred thousand results. In 2012 the United Nations General Assembly created a Conference on Happiness, published the *World Happiness Report*, and decreed that March twentieth would be annually observed as the International Day of Happiness. The most popular class in the history of Yale University is a class on happiness.[9] Given that happiness continues to preoccupy, what could be more important than to look at what the word meant when it was included with such prominence in the Declaration, how it was linked to liberty, and how the meaning of both of these words has changed since the eighteenth century? Modern definitions of happiness reference subjective emotional states such as joy, merriment, and cheerfulness. Within the brain, it is a limbic system (often called the mammalian brain) dominated experience. Dictionaries typically provide a dual definition for liberty that covers the political and social: (1) liberty is a state of freedom from a despotic government or foreign rule, and (2) liberty is the ability to choose and act freely. The four-note chord implies much more.

Chapters 3 through 5 will explore the lineage of this American genus of liberty. The founding period in America witnessed a confluence of four sources of influence: Greece, Rome, Christianity, and the Enlightenment. From the Athenians and Romans came the idea of the sovereignty of the people. Christianity placed the emphasis on the personal choice to be good and resist evil. In addition, the founding generation's views about the weaknesses inherent in human nature were drawn from Christianity. The Enlightenment thinkers focused on human progress based on man's ability to employ his capacity for reason.

Some of the framework for these chapters was built from Bernard Bailyn's influential and exhaustively researched book *The Ideological Origins of the American Revolution*. After extensive review of the speeches, meeting records, private and public documents, sermons, and—most ubiquitous of all—pamphlets, Bailyn discovered five basic sources for the colonial worldview that drove the moral and intellectual argument with Parliament. There must have been more going on that fueled their grievances, after all, when some of the most lightly taxed people in the western world would so vehemently object to Parliament's need to regulate the empire and pay off war debts by instituting a relatively mild tax policy. In ascending order of importance, they were: (1) classical antiquity, (2) the Enlightenment, (3) English common law, (4) New England Puritan theology, and (5) seventeenth and eighteenth-century English political theory that interpreted history as a never-ending battle between power and liberty. Since the English common law writers were products of the Enlightenment, I have condensed the sources of the genealogy of the four-note chord of liberty to four: Athens, the Roman Republic, Christianity, and the Enlightenment.

The reliance upon classical antiquity to bolster colonial arguments was common place. Pamphleteers would inevitably buttress their arguments and flaunt their intellectual credentials with the most wide-ranging array of classical analogies. The common practice of the day was to write under a classical pseudonym—Publius, Cato, Brutus—drawn from ancient Greece or Rome. Despite the wide-ranging scope of their classical references, the story that preoccupied the colonial writers was the collapse of the Roman republic. For the founders, the message from history was clear. The corruption that had led to the collapse of Roman liberty was analogous to the threats facing the colonists in the 1760s and 1770s. "They found their own provincial virtues—rustic and old-fashioned, sturdy and effective—challenged by the corruption at the center of power," wrote Bailyn, "by the threat of tyranny, and by a constitution gone wrong."[10] The history of Rome was more illustrative than determinative, for it was used to exemplify the points the colonists were making about their current conditions.

Historically and philosophically more important than the references to antiquity, were the founders' reliance on the Enlightenment writers, and the well-known lawyers from England's legal history. John Locke was the most frequently cited, often with great accuracy but at other times with less precision.[11] When referencing the great legal scholars such as William Blackstone or Edward Coke, the revolutionaries also tended to find different meaning depending on the positions they were arguing.[12] For the colonists, the Enlightenment philosophers and the English common law did not so much provide a precise blueprint for action as it was a way of putting their accumulated history into a broad philosophical context.

The fourth, and specifically American, tradition that influenced the founders' thinking about the supreme importance of their history can be traced back to the earliest years of New England settlement. Puritan theology inspired the colonists to think about the special role that America was playing in world history. It was a sweeping worldview that added a cosmic dimension to their political struggles. The settlement of America was directed by the hand of God to fulfill his goals for mankind. These early stirrings of what will later be captured in the phrase "manifest destiny," added a spiritual dimension that elevated the colonists' cause beyond provincial economic and political grievances. Though it initially stemmed from the austere Calvinism of New England, the spirit of the message was enlarged and modified by the entire range of American Protestantism.[13]

When knit together these principles became the all-encompassing theme of the American Revolution. History had demonstrated, and religion emphasized, that people were weak and prone to corruption. This pessimism was balanced with the Enlightenment belief in progress and the rational individual's ability to live free and flourish. People must remain vigilant to the never-ending tendency of the state to erode their liberty. In thoughts that would be articulated in the Declaration of Independence, government was perceived as potentially hostile to human liberty and should be overthrown if it exceeded its acceptable sphere of influence.

In summary, the founders perceived all actions originating from England's attempt to simply manage their expanded and debt-ridden empire (e.g., regulation of commerce, stationing troops, taxes) were nothing less than one more indicator of the fragility of liberty. Individual liberty was never safe for it existed in a continuous state of potential victimhood. Power in government was not inherently evil, for it had been legitimately created, in a Lockean sense, through a compact among citizens for mutual benefit. The danger was in the corruptibility, vanity, and selfishness of human nature.

The only thing that could assure the survival of liberty was the moral quality of the citizenry. It was the tendency for power to accumulate in one sector of society and crush the happiness and liberty of the citizens that was the never-ceasing problem for any form of government. Known since Aristotle, and such common knowledge that "the veriest smatterer in politics," wrote a Virginian in 1774, "must long since have had them all by rote,"[14] monarchy, aristocracy, or democracy would degenerate into tyranny, oligarchy, or mob-rule if their powers were not held in check. The mechanics for keeping power in check would be the Constitution. No rulebook for government, however, would ever resolve the central problem for the survival of liberty. Without the inner strength to stay the course of virtuous behavior, liberty would be short lived.

Chapter 6 will be a transition from the philosophical to the more personal by taking a closer look at Jefferson and Benjamin Franklin. In this book I am presenting the case that the founders believed that the survival of liberty was dependent on the moral virtue of the citizens. If this was true, there must be evidence that they worried about this problem on a personal level. This chapter will therefore be an up-close look at Jefferson and Franklin's struggles with self-mastery that was required for one to be truly free.

Self-government was not just a political concept, it was a psychological concept as well. Man was not meant to be controlled by a tyrant; either the one that rules the state, or the force that moves a person to be immoral and irrational. Of particular interest will be the evidence of Franklin and Jefferson's efforts at moderation. The importance of moderation must not be overlooked, wrote the political philosopher Thomas Pangle, "for no moral virtue receives such regular and oft-repeated praise from the *Federalist;* and no virtue had been accorded an equal importance in the *Spirit of the Laws,* the work to which the new Publius refers more often than to any other."[15] This is the concept that has been lost—and is most in need of revival—from our modern idea of liberty.

The heart of the debate over the structure of government that has been preserved in *The Federalist Papers* and the antifederalist speeches and articles, was the assumption that good government created and preserved the conditions under which liberty may be ensured. Chapters 7 and 8 will be an overview of the debate over our nation's second attempt at government: The Constitution. In the justification for a new constitution, there was a subtle loosening of the connection between virtue and liberty. An energized group (they were eventually labeled "Federalists") were somewhat less than encouraged by the initial results of the great American experiment in democracy. The unbounded optimism that liberty would flourish under the very lightest touch of government had begun to fade. Perhaps the common man was not quite virtuous enough, for events seemed to indicate that they were not electing good people to run the state governments. Americans were in need of more government at the national level, and less capable of true self-government at the state level.

In the minds of many, a new system was needed that would keep the bad people from doing so much harm. As John Marshall, the future chief justice who worked to strengthen the national government in the early decades of this nation, wrote immediately before the Constitutional Convention, "I fear . . . that those have truth on their side who say that man is incapable of governing himself."[16] Chapter 9 will bridge the founding generations' hopes for liberty with the present. Guided by Alexis de Tocqueville, some of the causes for the changes in our understanding of liberty will be considered. The modern conception of liberty has become highly individualized and happiness is now an emotional state that can only be subjectively assessed.

The narrative of American history has been a repudiation of the founders' belief in limited government made possible by a virtuously self-regulating and public-spirited citizenry. Gone from the political dialog is the irrevocable link between liberty and virtue. It is the abandonment of the value placed on virtue and the belief in moderation that is particularly troublesome. "We may look up to Armies for our Defense, but Virtue is our best Security," Sam Adams wrote in 1775, "it is not possible that any State should long remain free, where Virtue is not supremely honored." When it came to virtue, the founders did not believe that the private and the public were hermetically sealed off from one another. In the letter cited above, Adams wrote, "He who is void of virtuous Attachments in private Life, is, or very soon will be void of all Regard for his Country. There is seldom an Instance of a Man guilty of betraying his Country, who had not before lost the Feeling of moral Obligations in his private Connections."[17]

We are no longer concerned with what type of person is capable of participating in self-government. In Pericles' Funeral Oration, what every educated child of the founders' generation would have been familiar, virtue was central to Athenian success. Athenians possessed a "native spirit" and "cultivate refinement without stinting and knowledge without effeminacy; wealth we employ more for use than for show, and place the real disgrace of poverty not in owning to the fact, but in declining to struggle against."[18] Today the dialog focusses on whether the government allows each person enough liberty to make their own choices based upon personal values and their own self-established end states. When the founders thought about liberty the values were clearly established and the end state was well understood. They preached moderation and debated sumptuary laws; we glorify excess. Or as Aristotle might have put it, we have lost the habit of virtuous behavior.

Liberty has become morally neutral. A person is free to choose what they value and no one should be encumbered by another's vision of the good life. Do your own thing. Speak your own truth. Find yourself. Find your bliss. These are the mantras of the postmodernist era. The Enlightenment promised that the scientific method would reveal all the truths of nature, we know that science has not delivered. Any statement today that includes "self-evident," Jefferson's beloved phrase from the Declaration, ignites our suspicion. The assertion of self-evidence implies that the discussion is closed. The more knowledge accumulated in the fields of cosmology, physics, and neuroscience seems to dim rather than illuminate the Enlightenment belief that nature was orderly and intelligible. If there is anything that history should teach it is that there are no universally agreed upon self-evident truths. Anyone's truth statement is ultimately a personal perspective; a decision about what evidence to attend to.

The idea that self-government ensured liberty, but that self-government was dependent on virtue has been displaced by a glorification of wealth and power—being a winner! Madison wrote that "virtue is the vital principle of a republic, and it cannot long exist without frugality, probity, and strictness of morals."[19] Yet today virtue is so far gone from our modern theory of liberty that we no longer mourn the loss. We celebrate the unfettered expansion of personal liberty that is allowed by the lifting of traditional limits. On the other hand, government has assumed the responsibility of assuring that people live under the proper conditions to feel free. Liberty has been paradoxically both privatized and become the public responsibility.

In George Washington's first inaugural address, he emphasized the vital connection between the public good and virtue. He expressed confidence that "no separate views or party animosities" would prevent them from forming national policy on "the pure and immutable principles of private morality."[20] Americans must remember, wrote Washington, that "there is no truth more thoroughly established than that there exists in the economy and course of nature an indissoluble union between virtue and happiness; between duty and advantage; between the genuine maxims of an honest and magnanimous policy and the solid rewards of public prosperity and felicity."[21] Washington hoped that the citizenry would always remember that "we ought to be no less persuaded that the propitious smiles of Heaven can never be expected on a nation that disregards the eternal rules of order and right which Heaven itself has ordained."[22]

"It is possible to piece together a relatively coherent picture of what our Founders meant by liberty," wrote Georgetown University Professor George Carey, "what they believed its sources to be, and where they differed concerning its limits."[23] They knew what the word meant and were energized by the immediacy of the need to apply their unique awareness of liberty to alter the course of history. That is the problem I have set out to address. The founders knew that character mattered. Otherwise, a free people cannot long remain free. As the American people have been faced with new challenges, the need to continually restate and explain this truth has been neglected. The great philosopher, economist, and defender of liberty F. A. Hayek wrote, "if old truths are to retain their hold on men's minds, they must be restated in the language and concepts of successive generations. What at one time are their most effective expressions gradually become so worn with use they cease to carry a definite meaning."[24]

NOTES

1. "From Thomas Jefferson to Roger Chew Weightman, 24 June 1826," *Founders Online*, National Archives, version of January 18, 2019, https://founders.archives.gov/documents/Jefferson/98-01-02-6179.
2. "Abigail Adams to Thomas Jefferson, 6 June 1785," *Founders Online*, National Archives, version of January 18, 2019, https://founders.archives.gov/documents/Adams/04-06-02-0060-0001.
3. "From Thomas Jefferson to John Taylor, 4 June 1798," *Founders Online*, National Archives, version of January 18, 2019, https://founders.archives.gov/documents/Jefferson/01-30-02-0280. [Original source: *The Papers of Thomas Jefferson*, vol. 30, 1 January 1798–31 January 1799, ed. Barbara B. Oberg. Princeton: Princeton University Press, 2003, pp. 387–90.]
4. "From Thomas Jefferson to George Rogers Clark, 25 December 1780," *Founders Online*, National Archives, version of January 18, 2019, https://founders.archives.gov/documents/Jefferson/01-04-02-0295. [Original source: *The Papers of Thomas Jefferson*, vol. 4, 1 October 1780–24 February 1781, ed. Julian P. Boyd. Princeton: Princeton University Press, 1951, pp. 233–38.]
5. "From Thomas Jefferson to James Monroe, 24 October 1823," *Founders Online*, National Archives, version of January 18, 2019, https://founders.archives.gov/documents/Jefferson/98-01-02-3827.
6. Thomas Jefferson, "Query VIII. Population," Notes on the State of Virginia to *The Portable Thomas Jefferson*, ed. Merrill D. Peterson (New York: Penguin Books, 1977), 125.
7. Lochner v. New York, 198 Justia: US Supreme Court (April 17, 1906). Accessed January 24, 2019. https://supreme.justia.com/cases/federal/us/198/45/#tab-opinion-1921257.
8. Ibid.
9. David Shimer, "Yale's Most Popular Class Ever: Happiness," *New York Times*, January 26, 2018, https://www.nytimes.com/2018/01/26/nyregion/at-yale-class-on-happiness-draws-huge-crowd-laurie-santos.html.
10. Bernard Bailyn, *The Ideological Origins of the American Revolution*, fiftieth anniversary edition. ed. (Cambridge, MA: Belknap Press of Harvard University Press, 2017), 26.
11. Ibid., 28.
12. Ibid., 31.
13. Ibid. 32
14. Quoted in Bailyn, 70.
15. Pangle, *The Spirit of Modern Republicanism*, 89.
16. Quoted in Edward S. Corwin, *John Marshall and the Constitution A Chronicle of the Supreme Court*, ed. Allen Johnson, Gerhard R. Lomer, and Charles W. Jefferys, Abraham Lincoln ed., vol. 16, *The Chronicles of America Series* (New Haven: Yale University Press, 1919), 35, eBook presented by Project Gutenberg, http://www.gutenberg.org/files/3291/3291-h/3291-h.htm.
17. "Samuel Adams to James Warren—1775," Samuel Adams Heritage Society, last modified 2013, accessed September 4, 2016, http://www.samuel-adams-heritage.com/documents/samuel-adams-to-james-warren-1775.html.
18. Quoted in Carl J. Richard, *Greeks and Romans Bearing Gifts: How the Ancients Inspired the Founding Fathers* (Lanham, MD: Rowman & Littlefield Publishers, 2008), 58–59.

19. James Madison, quoted in Michael J. Sandel, *Democracy's Discontent: America in Search of a Public Philosophy* (Cambridge, MA: Belknap Press of Harvard University Press, 1996), 126.

20. *My Fellow Americans: Presidential Inaugural Addresses, from George Washington to Barack Obama* (St. Petersburg, FL: Red and Black Publishers, 2009), 7.

21. Ibid.

22. Ibid.

23. George Carey, "Eighteenth Century: American Contributions," in *An Uncertain Legacy: Essays on the Pursuit of Liberty*, ed. Edward B. McLean (Wilmington, DE: Intercollegiate Studies Institute, 1997), 112.

24. Friedrich A. Hayek, *The Constitution of Liberty: The Definitive Edition*, ed. Ronald Hamowy (Chicago: University of Chicago Press, 2011), 47.

ONE
The Four-Note Chord of Liberty

Four principles were knit together that shaped the founders' view of liberty: (1) personal liberty—the ability to do as one pleases within the rule of law, (2) political liberty—the right to participate in the government that makes those laws, (3) internal liberty—the ability to gain control over passions and destructive impulses that prevent a person from making good choices and passing good laws, and (4) public good liberty—a benevolent concern for the community. To help understand how this worked, I like to think of this metaphorically as a four-note musical chord. Each of the four components can be thought of as one note in the chord. To extend the musical metaphor, just as various sound vibrations are related to different emotional states, different conceptions of liberty can lead to dissimilar end states. The notes may be played separately, but when heard together it is a qualitatively different experience: a happy life.

Properly experienced, liberty led to a harmony within the person and a consonance within the community. Liberties were not just "things" that citizens possessed; with each deciding on their own what to do with their freedom irrespective of moral judgment or the greater good. Liberty to simply "do your own thing" was liberty misunderstood. Montesquieu—one of the founders' favorite political philosophers—wrote, "liberty in no way consists of doing what one wants . . . liberty can consist only in having the power to do what one should want to do and in no way being constrained to do what one should not want to do."[1] Or as Cicero—another favorite—wrote, "a very distinguished philosopher, was once asked what his pupils achieved, he answered that they learned to do of their own free will what the laws would compel them to do."[2] For the founders, the goal of liberty was nothing less than this: to elevate the human condition. One of the central pillars of the Enlightenment was the belief in progress based on reason. The founders were engaged in a project so much more important than just creating a new nation. They believed that the American people would experience a level of human flourishing that had never been experienced before. It would catch on, and all mankind would be elevated.

For these men of the Enlightenment, the ideal of moderation was the essential feature of the intelligent life. From the philosophers of antiquity to the Enlightenment, moderation was the cardinal trait for the achievement of the good life. Personal liberty without internal liberty could lead to extravagance, wastefulness, and licentiousness—a generally disordered life. If one lacked the understanding of when not to act, then liberty simply collapsed into personal chaos. Neuroscientists know that the balance between action and restraint is true down to the smallest unit of behavior—the firing of the neuron. There can be no behavior if neurons do not fire; but in many instances the inhibition of action requires more brain energy. The crowning achievement of human evolution is the ability of the mature and fully functioning frontal cortex to moderate behavior by inhibiting immediate impulses.

The founders were astute students of human nature and knew that passion was stronger than reason and a propensity toward excess was more typical than a tendency toward moderation "Will you tell me how to prevent riches from becoming the effects of temperance and industry" wondered John Adams "will you tell me how to prevent riches from producing luxury . . . will you tell me how to prevent luxury from producing . . . extravagance Vice and folly?"[3] It would require a constancy of effort that the American people should be able to accomplish. Participatory government had everywhere failed; in America it might be different. On this "vast Continent unpeopled, with Every advantage of Clymate, Soil, and Situation, for the Accommodation of human Life and the Enjoyment of Liberty," Adams wrote, "Where Despotism and Superstition have not established their Thrones" an elevated spirit of public good that was morally and politically superior to individual needs and selfish passions should prevail.[4] The political theorist Thomas Pangle wrote, "the American Founding came to be dominated by a small minority of geniuses who seized the initiative not merely by conciliating and reflecting common opinion but also by spearheading new or uncommon opinion."[5] What was particularly new and uncommon was their hope that an American style of liberty would take root, blossom, and flourish. America provided a fresh start for humanity. There would be more personal and political liberty than had ever been permitted to the citizens at any previous time in history. The individual state constitutions, the Articles of Confederation, and the Constitution all in turn spelled out how political liberty would be structured. The Bill of Rights protected personal liberty. Yet much more was going to result from this American experiment.

The protection of personal and political liberty was not just the goal of government: it was the means to a grander end. What I have labeled internal and public good liberty would thrive. Citizens, both as voters and representatives, who had mastered the personal struggle against weakness and corruption would make wiser political decisions and experience greater social agreeableness. The goal of a minimally intrusive government could be achieved through the promotion of this virtue-based liberty. People cannot be made good by laws, but without good people you cannot have good laws. Citizens would understand that liberty was to be experienced not by everyone just "doing their own thing" within the boundaries established by law, but by learning to live virtuously, and by becoming more fully actualized human beings through commitment to the public good. Folks would be happy.

In a letter to the Massachusetts militia, Adams wrote that if the people of America should start speaking about justice and moderation "while it is practicing Iniquity and Extravagance" and should pretend to manners of "frankness & sincerity while it is rioting in rapine and Insolence: this Country will be the most miserable Habitation in the World." The government they had created had no power to contend with unbridled passions. "Immorality," continued Adams "would break the strongest Cords of our Constitution as a Whale goes through a Net."[6]

WORD METAMORPHOSIS

Words give us access to human consciousness; but they are troublesome. With language there is always the gap between a speaker's intention and a listener's perception, as well as the fact that a single word may never adequately express a complex network of thoughts. James Madison, one of the great wordsmiths of the founding generation, wrote of the limitations of our language in *Federalist No. 37*:

> The use of words is to express ideas. . . . But no language is so copious as to supply words and phrases for every complex idea, or so correct as not to include many, equivocally denoting different ideas. Hence it must happen, that however accurately objects may be discriminated in themselves, and however accurately the discrimination may be conceived, the definitions of them may be rendered inaccurate, by the inaccuracy of the terms in which it is delivered. And this unavoidable inaccuracy must be greater or less, according to the complexity and novelty of the objects defined. When the almighty himself condescends to address mankind in their own language, his meaning, luminous as it must be, is rendered dim and doubtful, by the cloudy medium through which it is communicated.[7]

No words matter more than the ones that are meant to capture the most elusive and complex of our mental constructs. The philosopher Isaiah

Berlin wrote that "almost every moralist in human history has praised freedom. Like happiness and goodness, like nature and reality, the meaning of this term is so porous that there is little interpretation that it seems able to resist."[8] One problem that is generally overlooked is that in typical usage the words liberty and freedom are used interchangeably, depending on how they seem to fit in the flow of a sentence. In the Declaration, the great stylist of the written word Thomas Jefferson began with the claim that liberty was an inalienable right and closed with an assertion about a right to be free. Most writers use the words freedom and liberty interchangeably (as I have done) because they are generally understood as meaning the same thing. While it is agreed that liberty and freedom are synonymous, they have different origins.

A look back at the different experiences that these words were originally intended to capture provides credence to some of the ideas in this project. The fullest experience of liberty is not a solo experience; it happens in a social context. Liberty originated from the Latin word *libertas* which meant unrestricted by restraint. Freedom has an altogether different origin. It comes from a set of ancient northern European languages. Whether it be the English word *free*, the Norse *fri*, the German *frei*, the Dutch and Flemish *vrij*, the Celtic *rheidd*, and the Welsh *rhydd*; they all have the same unexpected root. They come down from the Indo-European *priya, friya,* or *riya*, which meant dear, beloved, or friend. To be free meant that a person was joined to a community of similar thinking people by ties of kinship and rights of belonging.[9]

It appears as though liberty and freedom, those two interchangeable words, as originally understood may actually pull us in opposing directions. The origin of liberty implied independence. Freedom, on the other hand, involved connectedness. However, these experiences do not need to cancel each other out. The founders did not think so. Their vision of a free society was not one where the personal, political and social were separate categories. Personal freedom functioned best within the context of community connections that nourished virtuous behaviors and wise political participation—the four-note chord.

It is interesting that some of the most influential liberty theorists have continued to subdivide the word into two forms. Isaiah Berlin, writing in the hot days of the Cold War, advanced a model of negative and positive liberty:

> The first of these political senses of freedom or liberty . . . I shall call the "negative" sense, is involved in the answer to the question, "What is the area within which the subject—a person or group of persons—is or should be left to do or be what he is able to do or be, without interference by other persons?" The second, which I shall call the positive sense, is involved in the answer to the question, "What, or who, is the source of control or interference that can determine someone to do, or be, this rather than that?"[10]

In this project, personal and internal liberty capture the idea of Berlin's negative and positive liberty respectively. Personal liberty (Berlin's negative liberty) means freedom of choice. It implies the absence of obstacles when making choices that promote one's self interest: live where you choose, marry whom you want, attend the church of your choice, and speak your own mind. With this type of liberty, we are thinking about relations among people within a community. The first ten amendments to the Constitution are well-known examples of this freedom. Although "Congress shall make no law" that would interfere with certain freedoms, that did not mean that there would be no personal values that would determine good choices. Internal liberty (Berlin's positive liberty) points to the presence of something that helps to make a better choice, for their must be a best choice. That something is called virtue.

Benjamin Constant, the early nineteenth-century political philosopher, identified two different ways of thinking about liberty: the liberty of the ancients and the liberty of the moderns. Ancient Greece may have been the birthplace of democracy, but by modern standards it seems like a rather un-free place to have lived. War was not seen as an evil to be avoided if at all possible, and slavery was widespread. The liberty of the ancients was experienced as an obligation to take part in the activities of the polis (and thanks to the work carried on by the slaves, having the leisure time to fulfill the requirement). Citizens directly participated (not through representatives) because they were immediately impacted by the decisions. For example, a man would be compelled to fight in the war that the community voted for.

If ancient liberty meant that a citizen was free to be part of the state, modern liberty can be viewed as the right to be free from the state. The essence of modern liberty was individualism. This passage from Constant rings familiar because it captures the spirit of the American Bill of Rights:

> It is the right of everyone to express their own opinion ... to dispose of property.... To come and go without permission.... It is everyone's right to associate with other individuals, either to discuss their interests, or to profess religion ... to occupy their days or hours in a way which is most compatible with their inclinations and whims.[11]

Each type of liberty presented certain dangers. In ancient times there was no value placed on individual rights. The danger of modern liberty, wrote Constant, was that we can become too "absorbed in the enjoyment of our private independence."[12] As citizens spend more time pursuing their specific interests, they may lose interest in politics. The ones who wield power "are so ready to spare us all sort of troubles.... They will say to us: what, in the end, is the aim of your efforts, the motive of your labors, the object of all your hopes? Is it not happiness? Well, leave this happiness to us and we shall give it to you."[13] An emphasis on the individualism of modern liberty can therefore lead to a growth in government. This happened in the United States and is one of the challenges addressed in this book.

The founders understanding of liberty was an amalgam of these ideas about negative, positive, ancient, and modern liberty. Today we hear in our mind's ear only the single notes of personal and political liberty, with an emphasis on the former and a diminishment of the latter. Berlin's positive liberty—the something that was required for people to be able to make the right choices—has shifted from the founders' belief in virtue to the paternalistic national government. The founders' expectation that citizens would stay in close touch with their Congressional representatives has also not been fulfilled.

This shift in the understanding of liberty happened slowly. The two notes of personal and political liberty, played without the other two, leads to an overly individualistic and subjective approach to life that is a distortion of the Enlightenment thinking of the founders. The individualism of the Enlightenment led to political revolutions, the questioning of the moral authority of monarchs, and suggested new answers to how Christians should make claims about moral actions and belief in God. Enlightenment individualism, however, was balanced by a belief in the power of human reason to continue mankind on a trajectory of progress. The founders believed they were taking part in a revolution concerning liberty and happiness that was a culmination of three thousand years of human experience.

NOTES

1. Charles Louis de Secondat de Montesquieu, *The Spirit of the Laws*, ed. Anne M. Cohler, Basia C. Miller, and Harold S. Stone (Cambridge: Cambridge University Press, 2009), 155.
2. Marcus Tullius Cicero, *Cicero: On the Commonwealth and on the Laws*, ed. James E. G Zetzel (Cambridge: Cambridge University Press, 1999), 3.
3. "To Thomas Jefferson from John Adams, 21 December 1819," *Founders Online*, National Archives, version of January 18, 2019, https://founders.archives.gov/documents/Jefferson/98-01-02-0977.
4. "John Adams to Mathew Robinson-Morris, 14 March 1786," *Writings from the New Nation 1784–1826*, ed. Gordon S. Wood (New York: Library of America, 2016), 42.
5. Thomas L. Pangle, *The Spirit of Modern Republicanism: The Moral Vision of the American Founders and the Philosophy of Locke* (Chicago: University of Chicago Press, 1988), 1.
6. "From John Adams to Massachusetts Militia, 11 October 1798," *Founders Online*, National Archives, accessed April 11, 2019, https://founders.archives.gov/documents/Adams/99-02-02-3102.
7. George W. Carey and James McClellan, eds., *The Federalist: By Alexander Hamilton, John Jay and James Madison*, Gideon ed. (Indianapolis: Liberty Fund, 2001), 183.
8. Isaiah Berlin, *Isaiah Berlin: Two Concepts of Liberty* (New York: Oxford University Press, 1969), 15, originally published 1969 as *Four Essays on Liberty*.
9. David Hackett Fischer, *Liberty and Freedom* (Oxford: Oxford University Press, 2005), 5

10. Berlin, *Two Concepts of Liberty*, 15.
11. Benjamin Constant, "Benjamin Constant, from 'The Liberty of the Ancients Compared with the Liberty of the Moderns' (1819)," in *Freedom: A Philosophical Anthology*, ed. Ian Carter, Matthew H. Kramer, and Hillel Steiner (Malden, MA: Blackwell Publishing, 2007), 16.
12. Benjamin Constant, "Benjamin Constant, The Liberty of Ancients Compared with that of Moderns (1819)," Online Library of Liberty: A collection of scholarly works about individual liberty and free markets, accessed February 12, 2019, https://oll.libertyfund.org/titles/constant-the-liberty-of-ancients-compared-with-that-of-moderns-1819.
13. Ibid.

TWO

The American Creed

The Declaration of Independence is the most read, listened to, and celebrated of our nation's founding documents. Unfortunately, the common title for the Declaration is a misnomer and misdirects our attention. *The Unanimous Declaration by the Thirteen United States of America* is the title of the document at the National Archives. In some reprints the words Unanimous and Thirteen were dropped. Jefferson's original title was *A Declaration by the Representatives of the United States of America, in General Congress Assembled*. It would be more useful to call it the Declaration of Liberty for that was the cause that the founders were declaring. Independence was just the essential and unavoidable result of the call for freedom from British tyranny. Alexis de Tocqueville, the astute observer of the early United States, wrote that the American Revolution was "produced by a mature and thoughtful taste for liberty, and not by a vague and undefined instinct for independence."[1] In the Gettysburg Address, Abraham Lincoln directed the nation's attention to the Declaration's assertions of liberty and equality. A focus on independence, or a reminder of the right of a "people to dissolve the political bonds which have connected them with another" and assume "the separate and equal station to which the laws of nature and of nature's God entitle them," would have been awkward. That was what the Confederates were fighting for.

The principles put forth in the Declaration were not meant to be simple justifications for independence. Jefferson did not even mention the American colonies or Britain in the first two paragraphs. The moral principles contained in those magnificent two paragraphs were meant to be, as Jefferson wrote, "an expression of the American mind"[2] with universal application. The Declaration has continued to directly inspire freedom seekers, and not necessarily independence seekers, from around the world and from the most dissimilar political philosophies, such as the

French revolutionaries of 1789 to Ho Chi Minh. The first line of the Universal Declaration of Human Rights that was passed by the United Nations in 1948 mentions "inalienable rights" and continues to echo Jefferson's words when it states that everyone "has the right to life, liberty and security."

In June of 1776, Richard Henry Lee introduced to the Second Continental Congress the Resolution for Independence that concisely stated the facts: "That these United Colonies are, and of right ought to be, free and independent States, that they are absolved from all allegiance to the British Crown, and that all political connection between them and the State of Great Britain is, and ought to be totally dissolved." The revolutionaries, however, were not just political architects who were deconstructing one system and replacing it with another. They were political philosophers engaged with the biggest questions: What was the purpose of government? How are people supposed to live? That was why in May of 1776, when John Adams wrote the preamble to the resolution encouraging the colonies to form new governments, he reminded that government must preserve "internal peace, virtue, and good order."[3] When Thomas Jefferson was asked to draft a statement that would explain to mankind why the colonies were separating from England, he went well beyond Lee's straight forward statement to assert the cardinal truths concerning human values. To be free to pursue happiness was the ultimate purpose of life:

> We hold these truths to be self-evident, that all men are created equal, that they are endowed by their Creator with certain unalienable Rights, that among these are Life, Liberty and the pursuit of Happiness. — That to secure these rights, Governments are instituted among Men, deriving their just powers from the consent of the governed. — That whenever any Form of Government becomes destructive of these ends, it is the Right of the People to alter or to abolish it, and to institute new Government, laying its foundation on such principles and organizing its powers in such form, as to them shall seem most likely to effect their Safety and Happiness.

In the Declaration, the word "happiness" not only appeared two times — it was in fact the only impactful word to be employed twice — it was the climactic word that ended the sentences where it was used. As both a musician and an architect, Jefferson was acutely attuned to the importance of repetition. The rhythm and design of his sentences were well thought out. He understood the importance of placing the emphatic word at the end of the sentence. If we imagine Jefferson putting those two sentences to music, one can almost see the crescendo symbols beneath the two stanzas. As Jefferson's biographer Dumas Malone wrote: "He was a ready writer but he could also be a fastidious one, and he never weighed his phrases more carefully than now."[4] The Declaration underwent extensive editing before it was approved by Congress, with some twenty-six major alterations and two new paragraphs added. Jefferson's statements about rights and happiness, however, remained largely untouched.[5]

As asserted in the Declaration, we have many unalienable rights, hence the use of the phrase "among these;" but Jefferson chose the most fundamental to spell out. People must be able to preserve their life, they must be free to control the direction of their life, and if these two rights were secured, they would be able to pursue the ultimate goal of happiness. Life and liberty were the means to the end state of happiness. When Jefferson wrote of happiness, he presented what might initially appear to be a conflict over how happiness was connected to a meaningful life. It was potentially paradoxical because with the dual mentions in the opening paragraph of the Declaration, each time it seemed to present a different perspective.

In the first use of the word it appeared as though happiness was an individual and private matter in that all men were "endowed by their Creator with certain unalienable Rights," with the implication that the quest was undertaken by and for the benefit of the individual. As long as a person was in possession of his life and was at liberty, he could pursue his own idea of happiness. Toward the end of the paragraph the meaning shifts. Happiness was a goal that was to be achieved collectively through the community, and it was the government's responsibility. The Declaration stated that "the People" will create new governments "as to them shall seem most likely to effect their Safety and Happiness." It could not be a purely private and subjective matter if the ultimate goal of government was to secure happiness for the general population. If each person was at liberty to self-define his ideal end state then one person's idea of happiness might conflict with another's. In a situation where the maintenance of happiness was to be achieved by the collective action of government, there must be an agreed upon definition of this happiness experience that everyone was pursuing.

The notion that the people will create governments that will both ensure safety and promote happiness was yet another idea potentially loaded with problems. Since the inception of this nation, much of the political debate has been a wrangling over the problem of the seemingly zero-sum game between liberty and security. If all are completely free there is no security so we give up some liberty with the hopes of finding some security. How much freedom to give up for how much safeguarding? We have not answered that question. On the other hand, if the citizenry shared a vision of happiness that was based on an agreed upon definition of the good life that all clear-thinking people would choose, conflict would be minimal. This idea of a communal or public happiness was an idea that was expressed by Jefferson in one of his few published documents. In *A View of the Rights of British America* published in 1774,

Jefferson wrote of a peoples' right to "establish new societies, under which such laws and regulations as to them shall seem most likely to promote *public* happiness" (italics added).[6] The idea of happiness as a shared group experience draws us away from the modern self-directed understanding of the word. More on this in the next chapter.

Jefferson never clearly explained what or who inspired his use of the word "happiness." In fact, if Jefferson's use of the word was unusual, then we might be inclined to dismiss the usage and attribute it to some sort of Jeffersonian eccentricity. Its prominence in the Declaration, however, was far from a deviation from the norms of his day. Both before and after the printing of the Declaration, the word happiness was regularly used when discussing the goal of government. The strength of the Declaration was that it stated what everyone already agreed to be true. Jefferson wrote that his intention had been "Not to find out new principles, or new arguments, never before thought of, not merely to say things which had never been said before; but to place before mankind the common sense of the subject."[7] In his own prickly sort of way, John Adams wrote that the Declaration did not present any novel ideas, for "there is not an idea in it but what had been hackneyed in congress for two years."[8]

Happiness was a familiar theme in many of the writings of the day. The well-known Reverend Jonathan Mayhew of Boston preached in 1754 that the purpose of government was the happiness of men. Although Jefferson claimed not to have read his pamphlet, in 1764 James Otis wrote that the end of government was "to provide for the security, the quiet, and happy enjoyment of life, liberty, and property."[9] In 1765, the Continental Congress asserted, "that the increase, prosperity, and happiness of these colonies depend on the full and free enjoyment of their rights and liberties."[10] Jefferson most certainly read the widely circulated work written in 1768 by Joseph Priestly, a man he admired enormously. "That the happiness of the whole community is the ultimate end of government can never be doubted," wrote Priestly, "The great object of civil society is the happiness of the members of it, in the perfect and undisturbed enjoyment of the more important of our natural rights, for the sake of which, we voluntarily give up others."[11]

After Parliament responded to the 1774 Boston Tea Party by closing the harbor, Josiah Quincy wrote *Observations on the Act of Parliament Commonly Called the Boston Port-Bill*. This pamphlet was read throughout the colonies and was an important step toward unification. Quincy's main theme expanded upon what Jefferson had referred to as public happiness—that the utilitarian objective of civil society was "the greatest happiness of the greatest number."[12] In response to the congressional delegates looking for guidance in writing state constitutions, in April of 1776 John Adams wrote *Thoughts on Government*, where he asserted that "the happiness of society is the end of government."[13]

In the years immediately preceding the Declaration, numerous essays appeared in the *Virginia Gazette* with titles such as "The Pursuit of Happiness," "Happiness," "Essay on Happiness," and "The Character of the Happy Life." All of these essays connected happiness with virtue.[14] Fresh in Jefferson's mind as well, must have been the widely read and commented upon pamphlet *Considerations on the Nature and Extent of the Legislative Authority of the British Parliament*, written in 1774 by James Wilson, one of the most highly respected legal scholars in the colonies. He expressed ideas, as well as the paragraph structure, that will find their way into the Declaration:

> All men are, by nature, equal and free: no one has a right to any authority over another without his consent: all lawful government is founded in the consent of those who are subject to it: such consent was given with a view to ensure the happiness of the governed, above what they would enjoy in an independent and unconnected state of nature. The consequence is, that the happiness of the society is the first law of every government.[15]

The most frequently cited source for Jefferson's statement on rights was from his friend and fellow Virginian, George Mason. In June of 1776, the Virginia Constitutional Convention approved *A Declaration of Rights* that had been written by Mason:

> That all men are by nature equally free and independent and have certain inherent rights, of which, when they enter into a state of society, they cannot, by any compact, deprive or divest their posterity; namely, the enjoyment of life and liberty, with the means of acquiring and possessing property, and pursuing and obtaining happiness and safety.[16]

Mason's emphasis on happiness can be traced to an earlier reference from 1774, when he penned the *Fairfax County Resolves*. He wrote that people are only to be governed by laws passed by elected representatives, and that the laws must protect the "safety and happiness" of the community.[17] Virginia's *Declaration of Rights* appeared in the *Pennsylvania Gazette* on June 12, 1776, the same day Congress appointed the committee of five to write the Declaration. We will never know, but we might safely assume, that Mason's *Declaration of Rights* was discussed. What, after all, could have been of greater interest to Jefferson than what was coming out of the Virginia Constitutional Convention? It is likely that Mason's words were fresh in Jefferson's mind, and it is very possible that a copy of Mason's *Declaration* was close at hand.

The similarities between Mason's and Jefferson's declarations are striking. It is also interesting to explore the words that Jefferson decided to exclude or move around. Jefferson was making an important moral argument, but he was also striving for a felicity and lightness of style. Mason wrote of the rights of "pursuing and obtaining happiness and safety." Jefferson dropped safety, perhaps believing that safety was already covered by the right to preserve one's life and be happy. Later in the paragraph when discussing the goals of government, he mentioned safety, so he may have thought it not necessary to repeat a word that was so fundamental to what underpinned anyone's idea of the good life. Jefferson also seemed to believe that we have a right to *pursue* happiness, but no right to necessarily *obtain* it. Jefferson corrected Mason's error. It was entirely within a person's own power to become virtuous and no government could make sure a person obtained it.

Much has been written about why Jefferson dropped any reference to property when discussing unalienable rights. Most writers of the day generally included it. Jefferson never said, so we will never know. One argument is that Jefferson did not include it because he did not believe that property was unalienable. Our unalienable rights came from nature, so when Jefferson wrote in 1813 "it is a moot question whether the origin of any kind of property is derived from nature at all,"[18] he may have been explaining the omission. Or perhaps it was a matter of style as opposed to any specific intention to downplay the importance of property. In that the protection of life and safety required the protection of property it may have appeared redundant to write out property. To end the sentence with the ringing phrase "pursuit of happiness," rather than the more earthy "property," may have just sounded better to his discerning ear. It was the crescendo of the sentence. It was what life and liberty were all about. With this, Jefferson was reaching back to the Aristotelian view of happiness: it was a life well lived and dependent on a person's efforts at a virtuous life as well as the individual's ability to maximize inherent capacities.

Historians debate which philosophers influenced Jefferson more. Merrill Peterson wrote of Jefferson's affinity for Lord Shaftsbury, Francis Hutcheson, Henry Home, and Lord Kame.[19] Most *Declaration* scholars discern the clear influence of John Locke.[20] The notion that freedom and happiness were inseparably linked to the protection of property and was therefore the primary object of government was Locke's essential thesis.[21] Countering that position was Garry Wills who argued that it was not Locke but the Scottish Enlightenment philosopher, Francis Hutcheson, who influenced Jefferson the most. Hutcheson formulated a utilitarian approach to the science of happiness—the greatest happiness for the greatest number"—and explored ideas about virtue, benevolence, and man's innate moral sense.[22] In fact, Jefferson was never attached to any one philosophical creed. He drew from a deep well of often competing philosophical schools, such as the Cynics, Stoics, and Epicureans; he was fascinated by Socrates, Cicero, Seneca, and Tacitus.[23]

Yet if we look to Jefferson's own words, we find Aristotle at the top of the list. In 1825, the aging Jefferson recollected that when he wrote the Declaration he had been influenced by "the harmonizing sentiments of the day, whether expressed in conversation, in letters, printed essays, or in the elementary books of public right, as Aristotle, Cicero, Locke, Sidney, &c."[24] Even if we were to concede that Jefferson's list was chronological—ancient Greece, ancient Rome, Enlightenment—the preeminence of Aristotle's views on the connections between politics and ethics had a tremendous impact on the Enlightenment thinking that Jefferson assimilated and articulated.[25] The Declaration was the eighteenth-century culmination of two-thousand years of thinking about the human condition that begins with Aristotle's systematic presentation of his view that politics and ethics were not two distinctly separate areas of study.[26] According to Aristotle "We took the end of political science to be the chief good, and political science is concerned most of all with producing citizens of a certain kind, namely, those who are both good and the sort to perform noble actions"[27]

If not for Aristotle it was probable that happiness may not have taken on the central importance that it did in the eighteenth century. Aristotle aimed to discover what accounted for the differences among all things that existed in nature. His answer was that all things possess within themselves a unique principle of movement toward a specific goal. The essential point of the two greatest collections of his theories about the good life, the *Nicomachean Ethics* and *Politics*, was that happiness was the end state to which human life was designed. Contrary to what some of the greatest ethicist such as Immanuel Kant concluded, that "the concept of happiness is such an indeterminate concept that, although every human being wishes to attain this, he can never say determinately and consistently with himself what he really wished and wants,"[28] Aristotle systematically and with great practicality presented a definition of happiness.

Aristotle explained why it was the greatest good and how it was to be achieved, both individually and communally.[29] The dual usage of happiness in the Declaration, that it was postulated as both an activity and an end-state, makes Aristotelian sense. The exercise of human reason was the pinnacle human endeavor that would culminate in happiness. Chapter 3 will continue to flush out the impact of Aristotle's argument for happiness and how it influenced the founders' idea of liberty. I will also be looking at two other philosophers from classical antiquity who helped to shape the ideology of liberty: Epicurus, and Cicero. That had a particularly powerful influence on the founders is beyond dispute. Not only are the Declaration's assertions concerning natural law traceable to Cicero, but Jefferson's manner of underpinning his argument with the claim that "we hold these truths to be self-evident" reminds one of Cicero's statement that "all that is so obvious that the matter does not need to be debated."[30]

NOTES

1. Alexis de Tocqueville, *Democracy in America*, trans. James T. Schleifer, ed. Eduardo Nolla, English ed. (Indianapolis: Liberty Fund, 2012), 1:117.
2. "From Thomas Jefferson to Henry Lee, 8 May 1825," *Founders Online*, National Archives, accessed April 11, 2019, https://founders.archives.gov/documents/Jefferson/98-01-02-5212.
3. "V. Preamble to Resolution on Independent Governments, 15 May 1776," *Founders Online*, National Archives, version of January 18, 2019, https://founders.archives.gov/documents/Adams/06-04-02-0001-0006.
4. Dumas Malone, *Jefferson the Virginian*, vol. 1, *Jefferson and His Time* (Boston: Little, Brown and Company, 1948), 221.
5. Carl Becker, *The Declaration of Independence: A Study in the History of Political Ideas* (New York: Vintage Books, 1958), 151.
6. Thomas Jefferson, "A Summary View of the Rights of British America," 1774, in *The Portable Thomas Jefferson*, ed. Merrill D. Peterson (New York: Penguin Books, 1977), 4.
7. "From Thomas Jefferson to Henry Lee, 8 May 1825," *Founders Online*, National Archives, accessed April 11, 2019, https://founders.archives.gov/documents/Jefferson/98-01-02-5212.
8. Quoted in Becker, *The Declaration of Independence*, 151.
9. Howard Mumford Jones, *The Pursuit of Happiness* (Cambridge: Harvard University Press) 1953, 4.
10. "Resolutions of the Continental Congress October 19, 1765," The Avalon Project: Documents in Law, History, and Diplomacy, accessed March 7, 2018, http://avalon.law.yale.edu/18th_century/resolu65.asp.
11. Herbert Lawrence Ganter, "Jefferson's 'Pursuit of Happiness' and Some Forgotten Men," *The William and Mary Quarterly*, 2nd ser., 16, no. 4 (October 1936): 585.
12. Jones, *The Pursuit of Happiness*, 4.
13. Ibid.
14. Jean M. Yarbrough, *American Virtues: Thomas Jefferson on the Character of a Free People* (Lawrence: University Press of Kansas, 1998), 14
15. Becker, *The Declaration of Independence*, 108.
16. "Virginia Declaration of Rights," The Avalon Project: Documents in Law, History, and Diplomacy, accessed March 7, 2018, http://avalon.law.yale.edu/18th_century/virginia.asp.
17. "George Mason and Historic Human Rights Documents," Gunston Hall, Home of George Mason, accessed March 7, 2018, http://gunstonhall.org/georgemason/rights.html.
18. "Thomas Jefferson to Isaac McPherson, 13 August 1813," *Founders Online*, National Archives, accessed April 11, 2019, https://founders.archives.gov/documents/Jefferson/03-06-02-0322.
19. Merrill D. Peterson, *Thomas Jefferson and the New Nation: A Biography* (New York: Oxford University Press, 1970), 55.
20. See Carl Becker, *The Declaration of Independence: A Study in the History of Political Ideas* (New York: Vintage Books, 1958); Ronald Hamowy, "Jefferson and the Scottish Enlightenment: A Critique of Garry Will's Inventing America: Jefferson's Declaration of Independence," *The William and Mary Quarterly*, 3rd ser., 36, no. 4 (October 1979).
21. Charles Beard's 1913 classic, *An Economic Interpretation of the Constitution of the United States*, was one of the earliest and most influential proponents of the theory that the founders were most concerned with the problems associated with the distribution of property and that government's primary purpose was the protection of economic well-being.
22. Garry Wills, *Inventing America: Jefferson's Declaration of Independence* (Garden City, NY: Doubleday & Company, 1978). Francis Hutcheson, "Philosophiae Moralis

Institutio Compendiaria," ed. Luigi Turco, *Natural Law and Enlightenment Classics* (Indianapolis, IN: Liberty Fund, 2007).

23. Peterson, *Thomas Jefferson and the New Nation*, 49.

24. Thomas Jefferson, "From Thomas Jefferson to Henry Lee, 8 May 1825," *Founders Online*, accessed March 7, 2018, https://founders.archives.gov/documents/Jefferson/98-01-02-5212.

25. Garrett Ward Sheldon, "The Political Theory of the Declaration of Independence," in *The Declaration of Independence: Origins and Impact*, ed. Scott Douglas Gerber (Washington, DC: CQ Press, 2002), 16.

26. Malcolm Schofield, "Aristotle's Political Ethics," *The Blackwell Guide to Aristotle's Nicomachean Ethics*, ed. Richard Kraut (Malden, MA: Blackwell Publishing, 2006), 305.

27. Aristotle, *Nicomachean Ethics*, I.9.1099b29-32.

28. Immanuel Kant, *The Cambridge Edition of the Works of Immanuel Kant: Practical Philosophy / Transl. and Ed. by Mary J. Gregor. General Introduction.* Allen Wood, ed. and trans. Mary J. Gregor (Cambridge: Cambridge University Press, 1996), 70.

29. Mark A. Young, *Negotiating the Good Life: Aristotle and the Civil Society* (Aldershot: Ashgate, 2005), 15.

30. Cicero, *De Officiis*, 1.6.

THREE
The Classical Roots of Virtue

Latin is one of the least popular Advanced Placement classes offered by the College Board. There are nine SAT subject tests offered; Greek is not one of them. Evidently an appreciation for the classic languages is not necessary to the education of the twenty-first century student. This reality would shock, and perhaps confound, the founders. Compare those facts with the curriculum of study that Thomas Jefferson planned for Peter Carr, his fifteen-year-old ward and nephew:

> For the present I advise you to begin a course of ancient history, reading everything in the original and not in translations. . . . reading the following books in the following order. Herodotus. Thucydides. Xenophontis hellenica. Xenophontis Anabasis. Quintus Curtius. Justin. This shall form the first stage of your historical reading, and is all I need mention to you now. The next will be of Roman history. . . . In Greek and Latin poetry, you have read or will read at school Virgil, Terence, Horace, Anacreon, Theocritus, Homer. Read also Milton's paradise lost, Ossian, Pope's works, Swift's works in order to form your style in your own language. In morality read Epictetus, Xenophontis memorabilia, Plato's Socratic dialogues, Cicero's philosophies.[1]

This reading, by the way, was to be undertaken in his free time, when not otherwise occupied by regular school work or his recommended two hours of daily exercise. Jefferson also admonished the young man that the development of a virtuous heart must be his primary goal. "Encourage all your virtuous dispositions" Jefferson wrote "from the practice of the purest virtue you may be assured you will derive the most sublime comforts in every moment of life and in the moment of death."[2] These were not just high-sounding platitudes from an elder to a minor. It was serious and meaningful advice, for there was an imperative connection between studying the classics and understanding the necessity of virtue.

It was the foundation upon which the founders' worldviews about liberty was built.

"Ours are the only farmers who can read Homer" boasted Jefferson in 1787.[3] A time-consuming book to squeeze in between Bible reading and farm chores, but this generation of revolutionaries had a practical need for familiarity with the classics. It was not for room décor that educated men of the founding generation spent fortunes to fill their bookshelves with complete volumes of the ancient Greek and Roman classics. They kept "commonplace books" where they copied out long passages in Latin and Greek, adopted classical pseudonyms when they wrote for publication, and in their leisure time translated the classical writers for entertainment as well as to display social status and erudition.[4] It was not merely a desire to incorporate rigor and discipline into the educational system that the children of the well-heeled spent so much of the school day studying the great writers from antiquity, and were required to recite them for admission to college. Eighteenth-century Americans believed that these writings contained the instructions for success for how life was to be lived and government was to be constructed so that it would promote liberty and happiness.[5]

They studied with an intensity motivated by the Enlightenment belief that they could discover the truths that God had made available to the human mind. The lessons that the founders gleaned from the study of the classics was twofold: cautionary concerning their political systems and inspirational when it came to their philosophies regarding the good life. The central message was that the quality of the citizen participants in the great American experiment was key. The best government could only happen if the participants were made of superior stuff. Only through putting in the hard work to improve their character would citizens be ready to make good choices when participating in government, possess the wisdom to deliberate with fellow citizens, possess the moral strength to make virtuous decisions, and understand that the good life happens within a social context.

The scope of their classical studies was wide-ranging, yet there were three philosophers who were particularly influential to the founders: Aristotle, Epicurus, and Cicero. The recurrent emphasis that the founders placed on virtue and happiness directs our attention first to Aristotle and his explanation of the interrelatedness of those two values. Only a constancy of effort at leading a virtuous life would lead to genuine happiness. Virtuous behavior, according to Aristotle, was understood as the desirable middle way between extremes. Moderation was therefore the ultimate moral virtue. The ancient thinker to whom Jefferson claimed to hold in the highest regard was Epicurus.[6] Jefferson wrote that Epicurus gave us, "the most rational system remaining of the philosophy of the ancients, as frugal of vicious indulgence, and fruitful of virtue as the hyperbolical extravagancies of his rival sects." [7] The central tenet of Epicurus' ethical teachings—which brings us back to Aristotle—was the importance of moderation.

Cicero's influence was both direct and indirect. In a count of the citations in the political literature produced between 1760 and 1805, Cicero was cited more often than all other classical authors from Greece and Rome combined.[8] From the fourth to the nineteenth century it was believed that the proper education of children included, above all, two important books: the works of Cicero and the Bible.[9] Cicero's indirect influence on the founders was through his impact on John Locke (particularly in his respect for private property) and Montesquieu—two of the most significant Enlightenment philosophers for the founders. Cicero was not only one of the most widely read but his diverse career as philosopher, politician, rhetorician, and lawyer would have appealed to the pragmatic founders: he was one of their own as a man of action and not just words.

Each of these three philosophers dealt with the architectural framework of good government. They were concerned with the questions of who should participate in the governing of the political unit, and why. With the greatest questions before them—Why was rule by England wrong? What would be better?—it was natural for the founders to look to the classical philosophers who had been most preoccupied with the connections between how people organized their political space and human flourishing. Good government, however, was not the end; it was the means to an end. Only through a justly organized political system could human fulfillment be attained. The focus of this book is not on the structure of political regimes but on the human qualities that contribute to their failure or success. Therefore, I will primarily be looking at Aristotle's *Nicomachean Ethics*, an assortment of the letters written by Epicurus, and Book I of Cicero's *De Officiis*.

ARISTOTLE

The primacy of virtue as the essential ingredient for the experience of internal liberty, the survival of political liberty, and the fulfillment of public good liberty (three of the four notes in my metaphorical musical chord) can best be understood with Aristotle's teachings as a starting point. Aristotle wondered about everything. He invented deductive logic as a formal science and influenced ethics, politics, aesthetics, psychology, biology, and astronomy.[10] Many of his teachings are offensive to the modern reader (e.g., natural slavery, the inferiority of women, infanticide for population control), but his ideas about the good life and how civic virtue was essential to human flourishing should be of continuing significance. Circumstances and belief systems have certainly changed, but human nature not so much. Aristotle's explanation of why happiness was the ultimate goal of human life, and the methods for attaining that goal, infused the founders' beliefs about what was a life well-lived. To support and perpetuate the good life for each individual citizen was the ultimate goal of government.

The first problem to be confronted is one of translation. The Aristotelian meaning of happiness was different from how it is used today.[11] Dictionaries typically offer transitory feeling-state definitions of happiness such as "a pleasurable or satisfying experience" from Merriam-Webster; or "good fortune, pleasure, contentment, joy" from the Cambridge Dictionary. The Oxford Dictionary defines happiness as "good fortune or good luck," a suggestion that it is something that simply happens to a person. The etymology of the word is from the Old Norse and Old English word "hap" which meant chance or luck. *Hap*piness was something that was *hap*hazard or *hap*penstance; not something one could control. No modern dictionary connects happiness with moral correctness or ethical standards of right and wrong, yet that was what Aristotle (and the founders) had in mind. Aristotle used the word *eudaimonia*, and the word has lost its original connotation when translated into English as happiness.

The Greek word does not convey a state that was based in the unstable and subjective emotional realm. In fact, there is no single English word that completely captures the idea of *eudaimonia*. Words such as "self-actualization" or "flourishing" come close. Yet even those two words, which might imply a static state, fail to capture the full meaning. It was a dynamic experience of actively working toward becoming an excellent person. Nor does the modern idea of happiness include the idea of moderation. Emotional states are generally viewed on a continuum, and the synonyms for happiness such as joy, glee, or giddiness do not suggest a median point. Aristotle reasoned that true happiness was a character state—not an unstable emotional condition—that was marked by a person's ability to wisely choose the most composed responses to life's challenges. Human flourishing was inextricably connected to a life of studied moderation. This is what Aristotle meant by virtue. It was a disposition of character which resulted in a particular way of deliberating and choosing so that actions were undertaken for the right reason, at the right time, and for the right goal.[12]

The *Nicomachean Ethics* covered Aristotle's thoughts on human nature and provided the blueprint for how to build the happy life. It opened with an analysis of what Aristotle believed to be the central human problem: the longing for happiness and how it was to be obtained. There was practicality in this undertaking. According to Aristotle, this branch of philosophy was not abstract and theoretical, it was about how to be a good person.[13] Beginning from the premise that all actions and choices are aimed at some goal, there must be some clarity about what was the highest goal for humans. If you don't know where you are going, you probably won't get there. Aristotle believed that the highest goal we should be reaching for would be something that was uniquely fit for a human, once attained it would be hard to take away, and that it was not chosen because it would lead to something else but was intrinsically desirable. The ultimate goal of all human activity was clearly happiness.[14] All other goals are sought not for their own sake but because we think it will bring us happiness.

Aristotle's understanding of ultimate function was fundamental to his conclusions about happiness. All actions were undertaken with some unique purpose, so it followed that the human being must have some ultimate and unique purpose or function. The unique characteristic of humans was their ability to reason.[15] It therefore followed that if a person hoped to be the best he could be and to experience the most pleasure, he would strive to maximize this faculty. In other words, happiness was not just about getting what you want, but learning to want the right thing. Happiness was about "living well and acting well."[16] Or put more directly, "happiness is virtue."[17]

There were other pursuits that a person might wrongly believe would bring happiness such as sensual pleasure, wealth, and honor. Of the three, Aristotle was most critical of the life devoted purely to sensual pleasure. To lead such a life placed the human at an animal level of existence. We humans can certainly do better than live as a lizard basking in the sun or a pig rolling in mud. Wealth was not happiness, for money was acquired for the sake of obtaining something else. Money, after all, has no intrinsic value, can be easily squandered or lost, and the acquisition and enjoyment is dependent on others. The pursuit of honor was preferred over the other two, for to be truly honorable one must be virtuous. But honor was something that comes to us from others, so it could not be the ultimate goal. An additional benefit of finding happiness through a life of virtuous activity is that it would never lead to conflict with others. Happiness was the only goal that was complete in and of itself. The virtuous person "has no need of pleasure as some kind of lucky ornament . . . actions in accordance with virtue are pleasant in themselves."[18] Virtue was happiness, but it takes hard work to get there. Only as a result of a steady application of thought and effort could a person become habituated to behaving in a virtuous manner, thereby achieving the purest state of happiness.

Having established the important point that happiness was to be achieved through virtuous activity, Aristotle explored in great detail the specific types. There were two general categories of virtue: moral and intellectual. These virtues were not present by nature. The intellectual virtues were developed through teaching and the moral habits would be acquired through focused activity. The most important concept when it came to defining virtue and achieving happiness was the doctrine of the mean. A mean was a point of excellence between the two extremes of deficiency or excess; it was at that point—the Golden Mean—where virtue could be found. For example, an excessively fearful person is a coward and a person who fears nothing is reckless. The virtue of courage is acquired by understanding the middle path between the two.

The question that followed was how to discover the virtuous point between the extremes. Finding the mean, that point of excellence where virtue exists, was not a simple arithmetic problem. That good place was not the same for everyone; it happened on a sliding scale. Aristotle used the example of the famous sixth century athlete Milo to illustrate his doctrine of the flexibility of the mean. A little food for Milo would be a lot of food for another.[19] Excess or deficiency will always ruin the good, and the wise person will know how to find it. Virtue involved both emotions and behaviors. It was about knowing and wanting to do the right thing, at the right time, towards the right people. To identify the ideal middle point required the development of intellectual virtue. Through a constant application of effort and proper education the student of virtue would come to understand this basic truth: the happy life was not measured by having the most (e.g., rashness or self-indulgence), or the least (e.g., fear or lack of ambition), but in cultivating a habit of moderation.

Aristotle taught that people needed reasonably healthy and pleasurable lives, they needed to be able to figure out the right thing to do in given situations and have the moral strength to follow through, and they needed to be educated about virtue and develop it with correct practice. Yet that was not enough. The happy life was fulfilled within a social context. Aristotle's central argument was that happiness was the end to which all human activity was aimed: it was self-sufficient. However, the term self-sufficient can be misunderstood as it connotes a self-contained

Table 3.1. Aristotle's Virtues

Sphere of Action	Virtue	Deficiency	Excess
Fear and Confidence	Courage	Cowardice	Rashness
Pleasure and Pain	Temperance	Insensibility	Self-Indulgence
Proper Living	Benevolence	Stingy	Giving Too Much
Getting and Spending	Magnificence	Pettiness	Tastelessness
Feelings About Self	Pride	Pusillanimity	Vanity
Anger	Good Temper	Lack of Spirit	Irascibility
Self-Expression	Truthfulness	Mock Modesty	Boastfulness
Conversation	Wittiness	Boorishness	Buffoonery
Social Conduct	Friendliness	Cantankerousness	Obsequiousness
Shame	Modesty	Shamelessness	Bashfulness
Sight of Undeserved Good Fortune	Proper Indignation	Spite	Envy

individualism. Virtue was not private. Most of the virtues, after all, such as truthfulness or magnanimity, could only be realized through relationships with like-minded individuals. Just as the baseball player requires a team to play with, the virtuous person requires friends with whom to do good and achieve the happy life. Virtuous activity will be more continuous and enjoyable in the presence of other virtuous people.

Aristotle's belief that the virtuous life was best achieved within a social context is clarified by his examination of friendships. Just as there were many different ways that people have defined and pursued happiness, but only one best way, there were three hierarchical levels of friendship. The two lowest levels of friendship were based on usefulness or pleasure, and were selfish by definition. If one is working in an office it is useful to be friendly with the other people one sees every day. It is better to be on friendly terms with one's neighbors than not. If a person enjoys playing a sport that requires other participants such as tennis or golf, it is likely that he or she will develop friendships with other players. With these two types of friendships the ethical qualities of the other do not matter very much. One might find a person of very low character to be useful or entertaining.

The third type of friendship was about being connected with other virtuous people. The whole is greater than the sum of its parts in that individual capacities for happiness have expanded through the interactions of virtuous people in the community. The happy life was something that was larger than what individuals could attain on their own. Aristotle's notion about the virtuous person needing friendship was extended to include the idea of all citizens engaged in a cooperative endeavor toward the common good. Virtuous people were necessary for the maintenance of good government. In turn, good government would promote public-spirited characters.

EPICURUS

Aristotle had dismissed the pursuit of pleasure as the lowest level of human existence, so at first blush it would appear that his teachings would conflict with those of his younger contemporary Epicurus, whose ethical system was a way of life focused on pleasure. Once again, however, we begin with a problem of translation and original meaning. Just as the word happiness has come to mean something completely different from what it meant to Aristotle, the word "epicurean" does not mean today what it meant to the original followers of Epicurus. With modern usage, one might describe an epicurean as a person seeking the pleasurable life through luxurious living and indulgence in fine wine and gourmet food. To the contrary, Epicurus believed as did Aristotle, that through engaging the faculty of reason one would discover that moderation was the key to the good life. "One must reason about the real goal and every clear fact," Epicurus instructed his followers, "if not, everything will be full of indecision and disturbance."[20] The "real goal" in life was to master the appetites; as Epicurus wrote, "It is impossible to live pleasantly without living prudently, honorably, and justly and impossible to live prudently, honorably, and justly without living pleasantly."[21]

Although Jefferson was a connoisseur of French food and wine, this was not what he meant when he indicated that his favorite philosopher was Epicurus.[22] "I too am an Epicurian" Jefferson wrote to a longtime friend, for he gave us the best "laws for governing ourselves."[23] Epicurus taught that the goal of life was pleasure; yet this was not a "more is better" hedonistic definition of pleasure. Epicurus' life of pleasure was defined by a freedom from an agitated state that resulted from unlimited cravings. It was the happiness of equanimity. It was the happiness of self-control. It was the only way one could truly be free.

In an outline believed to have been written in 1799, Jefferson sketched out what he found most valuable in the doctrine of Epicurus. Jefferson wrote "that happiness was the aim of life, virtue was the foundation of happiness, utility was the test of virtue."[24] Even John Adams, who did not rate Epicurus as highly as did Jefferson, admitted that the philosopher's thoughts contained "a mixture of good morals, manly virtues & true opinions"[25] It was indeed Epicurus' teachings about ethics and virtue that are most relevant to the founders' vision. The cardinal virtues that Epicurus emphasized related to the self-restraint that is at the foundation of internal liberty: "prudence, temperance, fortitude, justice."[26]

The founders studied the classical writers because they believed, as quintessential men of the Enlightenment, that life as it was meant to be lived could be understood through thoughtful reasoning about human nature and from historical evidence. Moral values were to be based on the comprehension of the true and permanent essence of human nature—for that the founders had looked to the Greeks. Aristotle and Epicurus explained that the good life was dependent on self-regulation, the employment of reason, and the cultivation of virtue. Yet it was the style of government that had been implemented by the Romans that would permit the good life to be realized. The Roman Republic ultimately failed but that did not diminish the founders' powerful ideological link with Rome. They believed that the collapse had not been caused by an inherently weak design of the Republic but from a crisis in the character of the Roman people.

CICERO

From Jefferson's perspective, the Roman Republic was destroyed by "the most bitter factions and tumults" and a government controlled by "a heavy-handed unfeeling aristocracy over a people rendered desperate by poverty and wretchedness."[27] In America the context was entirely different and therefore the outcome might be different; for there was no historical aristocracy and the abundance of land and opportunity would allow for a republican style of government to flourish. This was the historic pivot upon which the founders placed all their hopes for the future of America. A Roman styled representative republic would only work if the citizens and their representatives understood the importance of virtuous living. As creators of a new system of representative government, the founders were drawn to the classical writer who offered the most insight on Roman decline, corruption, and decadence: Cicero

The founders knew that Cicero's misty-eyed and embellished portrayal of the collapsed Roman Republic was unrealistic, yet they projected his veneration of Rome's past on to their idealized future of the American Republic. Cicero attributed to the citizens of the Roman Republic a virtuous wisdom that the founders hoped would be revitalized in America. As Jefferson wrote to Adams in 1819, the letters of Cicero breathed "the purest effusions of an exalted patriot" although he doubted that the good government that Cicero had hoped to restore had ever actually existed in Rome. The Roman people, according to Jefferson, had never been "like ours, enlightened, peaceable, and really free . . . their people were so demoralized and depraved as to be incapable of exercising a wholesome controul."[28] Many years earlier, Adams had expressed similar thoughts when he wrote that "Cicero had the most Capacity and the most constant as well as the wisest and most persevering Attachment to the Republick." After rereading a book about the life of the great statesmen, Adams proclaimed that "I Seem to read the History of all ages and Nations in every Page, and especially the History of our own Country for forty years past."[29]

Cicero's major ethical work was *De Officiis*, which focused on the connection between the internal qualities of virtue and its external manifestations of social cohesion. In addition to the many activities he had carried out as a citizen of Rome, he hoped to introduce to his Latin readers the philosophy of the Greeks—most notably Aristotle. Ostensibly written as an extended letter of advice to his son who was studying in Greece, it was intended as instructions for the Roman governing class. Cicero's familiarity with the Greek philosophers was demonstrated through his discussion of how reason could lead people to appreciate what qualities were associated with a life well lived. The Aristotelian and Stoic influences were present in Cicero's discussion on the importance of engaging reason to control the unvirtuous impulses. Cicero wrote that the human spirit consisted of two parts: impulse and reason. Impulse "snatches a man this way and that;" reason prevents him from doing "anything for which he cannot have a persuasive justification."[30]

Rejecting the utilitarian approach that posits that the good or evil of an action was determined by its effects, Cicero wrote that the virtuous life was the highest good and was sought for its own sake. "The man who defines the highest good in such a way," wrote Cicero, that it has not connection with virtue, but is only concerned with his own advantage "cannot . . . cultivate either friendship or justice or liberality. There can certainly be no brave man who judges that pain is the greatest evil, nor a man of restraint who defines pleasure as the highest good."[31]

To want to discover truth was in the nature of mankind. Cicero wrote that "all of us feel the pull that leads us to desire to learn and to know; we think it a fine thing to excel in this, while considering it bad and dishonourable to stumble, to wander, to be ignorant, to be deceived."[32] There were four cardinal virtues that Cicero believed the pursuer of truth would discover. First there was the ability to perceive truth (wisdom); second was the ability to preserve good fellowship through respect of property and faithfully following through on agreements (justice); third was the strength of spirit (magnanimity); and fourth dealt with proper decorum "with order and limit in everything that is said and done (modesty and restraint are included here)."[33] Justice was the most important of the virtues for it was what allowed for there to be fellowship and held communal life together.[34] Cicero returned repeatedly to the importance of social cohesion and the necessity for men of good character to be focused on the public good. As Cicero explained, "we are not born for ourselves alone . . . , but our country claims for itself one part of our birth, and our friends another . . . everything produced on the earth is created for the use of mankind, and men are born for the sake of men, so that they may be able to assist one another."[35]

In chapter 2, the question was addressed whether happiness could plausibly be thought of as a private or subjective experience that everyone could pursue in their own idiosyncratic way. Aware of the intellectual connection that the founders maintained with the classical philosophers, it can be concluded that happiness was an objective experience that rational people would agree upon. The happy life was a virtuous and honorable life. In the Declaration of Independence, Jefferson had connected happiness with good order. Furthermore, it was an approach that would bind the community together. As Cicero wrote, expanding on the ideas he had gathered from Aristotle,

> For honourableness—the thing that I so often mention—moves us, even if we see it in someone else, and makes us friends of him in whom it seems to reside. (All virtue indeed lures us to itself and leads us to love those in whom it seems to reside, but justice and liberality do so the most.) Moreover, nothing is more lovable and nothing more tightly binding than similarity in conduct that is good. For when men have similar pursuits and inclinations, it comes about that each one is as

much delighted with the other as he is with himself; the result is what Pythagoras wanted in friendship, that several be united into one.[36]

Aristotle located virtue as the middle way between two behavioral extremes. Epicurus argued that moderate living was the key to the good life. Cicero, as well, emphasized the importance of moderation that was so important to eighteenth-century Americans. Cicero wrote that no one was perfectly wise and thoroughly virtuous, so we "must particularly foster those who are most graced with the gentler virtues, modesty, restraint, and the very justice which I have now been discussing at length. For a brave and great spirit in a man who is not perfect nor wise is generally too impetuous; but those other virtues seem rather to attach themselves to a good man."[37] This important connection between living virtuously and moderately that was important to eighteenth-century Americans will be explored on a more personal level in chapter 6.

NOTES

1. "From Thomas Jefferson to Peter Carr, 19 August 1785," *Founders Online*, National Archives, version of January 18, 2019, https://founders.archives.gov/documents/Jefferson/01-08-02-0319. [Original source: *The Papers of Thomas Jefferson*, vol. 8, *25 February–31 October 1785*, ed. Julian P. Boyd. Princeton: Princeton University Press, 1953, pp. 405–8.]

2. Ibid.

3. Thomas Jefferson, "Extract from Thomas Jefferson to St. John de Crèvecoeur (January 15, 1787)," Jefferson Quotes and Family Letters, accessed March 4, 2018, http://tjrs.monticello.org/letter/8.

4. Carl J. Richard, *Greeks and Romans Bearing Gifts: How the Ancients Inspired the Founding Fathers* (Lanham, MD: Rowman & Littlefield Publishers, 2008), 12–38.

5. Ibid., 179.

6. M. Andrew Holowchak, "The 'Reluctant' Politician: Thomas Jefferson's Debt to Epicurus," *Eighteenth-Century Studies* 45, no. 2 (2012): 277.

7. Thomas Jefferson, "Thomas Jefferson to Charles Thomson, 9 January 1816," *Founders Online*, accessed September 10, 2016, http://founders.archives.gov/documents/Jefferson/03-09-02-0216.

8. Donald S. Lutz, *A Preface to American Political Theory* (Lawrence: University Press of Kansas, 1992), 136.

9. Melissa Lane, "'Ancient Political Philosophy,'" ed. Edward Zalta, *The Stanford Encyclopedia of Philosophy* (Summer 2017 Edition), https://plato.stanford.edu/archives/sum2017/entries/ancient-political/.

10. Jonathan Jacobs, *Aristotle's Virtues: Nature, Knowledge, and Human Good* (New York: Peter Lang, 2004), 2.

11. In fact, Aristotle's usage of the word represented a shift from an earlier understanding. The word is a compound of the prefix "eu"—meaning well—and "daimōn"—which referred to a spirit guide. For example, according to Plato, Socrates claimed his daimōn warned him of potential mistakes, though never gave him advice about what course of action to take. This would imply that a state of eudemonia would be influenced by forces outside of the person.

12. Aristotle, *Nicomachean Ethics*, II.6, 1106b17–23

13. Ibid., II.2, 1003b26–20.

14. Ibid., I.7, 1097b1–6.

15. Ibid., I.7, 1098a7–8.

16. Ibid., I.8, 1098b21–22.
17. Ibid., I.8 1098b31.
18. Ibid., I.8, 1099a16–23.
19. Ibid., II.8, 1106b 1–8.
20. Brad Inwood and Lloyd P. Gerson, trans., *The Epicurus Reader: Selected Writings and Testimonia* (Indianapolis: Hackett, 1994), 32.
21. Ibid.
22. Richard, *The Founders and the Classics*, 187.
23. Thomas Jefferson, Jefferson to William Short, 31 October 1819, Merrill D. Peterson, *The Portable Thomas Jefferson* (Harmondsworth, Eng.: Penguin Books, 1977), 564–65.
24. Thomas Jefferson, "Notes on the Doctrine of Epicurus, [ca. 1799?]," *Founders Online*, accessed September 10, 2016, http://founders.archives.gov/documents/Jefferson/01-31-02-0241 .
25. John Adams, "From John Adams to John Rogers, 6 February 1801," *Founders Online*, accessed September 10, 2016, http://founders.archives.gov/documents/Adams/99-02-02-4799.
26. Inwood and Gerson, *The Epicurus Reader*, vii.
27. Thomas Jefferson, "Notes on the State of Virginia," *The Portable Thomas Jefferson*, ed. Merrill D. Peterson (New York: Penguin Group, 1977), 175.
28. Lester J. Cappon, ed., *The Adams-Jefferson Letters: The Complete Correspondence between Thomas Jefferson and Abigail and John Adams*, 1959 ed. (Chapel Hill [u.a.]: University of North Carolina Press, 2001), 549.
29. "From John Adams to Benjamin Rush, 4 December 1805," *Founders Online*, National Archives, accessed March 7, 2018, last modified March 30, 2017, https://founders.archives.gov/documents/Adams/99-02-02-5110.
30. Cicero, *De Officiis*, 1.101.
31. Ibid., 1.5.
32. Ibid., 1.17.
33. Ibid., 1.15.
34. Ibid., 1.20.
35. Ibid., 1.23.
36. Ibid., 1.56.
37. Ibid., 1.46.

FOUR
Greek Eleutheria and Roman Liberatas

The word *democracy* originates from the Greek word *demokratia* which translates to "people power." The theory of balanced government was an inheritance from the Romans. Ancient Athens and Rome were also where the earliest recognition of a nascent concept of personal liberty emerged. Political and personal liberty were the two foundation stones of American politics; nonetheless, the founders were harsh critics as they mined the writings of the classical Greeks and Romans for evidence of the weaknesses that led to their failures. Athens with its demagogues was a model for how participatory government had been chronically unstable, and how free citizens can become unruly mobs led by devious and manipulative men grasping for power and wealth. The Romans ultimately traded the political and economic disorder of their republic for the relative stability of rule by an emperor.

In his monumental analysis of history, philosophy, and government, John Adams reflected that Athenian democracy was never simple and it never really worked. Dictators and ruling assemblies "produced a never-ending fluctuation in the national councils, continual factions, massacres, proscriptions, banishment, and death of the best citizens: and the history of the Peloponnesian War by Thucydides, will inform us how the raging flames at last burnt out."[1] Jefferson wrote that there was little to be learned from studying the politics of the classical Greeks because they "had just ideas of the value of personal liberty but none at all of the structure of government best calculated to preserve it." The development of representative political institutions "has rendered useless almost everything written before on the structure of government and in a great measure relieves our regret if the political writings of Aristotle, or of any other ancient, have been lost, or are unfaithfully rendered or explained to us."[2]

There was little that Jefferson thought that Alexander Hamilton would have agreed with, but he concurred with Jefferson's conclusions about the failures of ancient political systems. It was "impossible to read the history of the petty republics of Greece and Italy" wrote Hamilton, "without feeling sensations of horror and disgust at the distractions with which they were continually agitated, and at the rapid succession of revolutions, by which they were kept perpetually vibrating between extremes of tyranny and anarchy."[3] Yet despite history's failures, the founders did not believe they were building houses on sand. The idea was good. The people had gone wrong. The ancients gave to posterity the greatest gift: the belief in the sovereignty of the people. The Americans would show mankind how to make it last.

For the founders had also inherited from the Greeks and Romans the idea that liberty can only be promoted and stabilized by virtue. The founders were Enlightenment thinkers who were constructing evidence based political theories built from established truths about ethical behavior. They were not, however, reconstructing the classical political systems. Madison wrote that the people of America "have paid a decent regard to the opinions of former times and other nations, they have not suffered a blind veneration for antiquity."[4] History was a "laboratory in which the autopsies of the dead republics would lead to a science of social sickness and health" wrote the historian Gordon Wood.[5] The founders believed that America would be the wellspring for the revitalization of the principle that true liberty must be cultivated with good character. American citizens would enjoy personal freedom, be involved in government, and be committed to the welfare of the community; all sustained by a constancy of effort to live a morally righteous life.

As products of the Enlightenment, the founders believed in progressively evolving constitutionalism that was based on ideas about limited government, with separate and balanced institutions that existed by consent of the governed, and the existence of natural law. They held that these ideas originated in antiquity and were restored by the Enlightenment philosophers.[6] Though the actual historic evidence does not always agreeably fit with the conclusions, the history of western civilization—idealized, abridged, and contorted as it may have been—was important because it fit with the founders' view that they were engaged in a project that was the culmination of western civilization.[7]

GREEK ELEUTHERIA

Granted that the emergence of any abstract idea that originated in antiquity will remain mysterious to some degree, the founders generally began with the early history of Athens. Although the ancient Greeks had little conception of personal liberty as it is understood today, the earliest seed of the idea of an unalienable right to freedom was planted during the sixth century BC under the leadership of Solon. With the rise of commerce, trade and the increasing problems of debt bondage, Solon was the first to introduce the idea of an unalienable right to freedom.[8] Solon forbade citizens from selling themselves into slavery to pay off a debt. Plutarch wrote, "the first thing which he settled was . . . no man, for the future, should engage the body of his debtor for security."[9] An Athenian who had fallen on hard times was not to be oppressed or tyrannized by the wealthy. Cleisthenes is known as "the father of Athenian Democracy," who with the support of the middle class, reformed the constitution and established equality among citizens in the years 508–507 BC.

The way in which freedom was first connected to slavery is essential to understanding the origins of this concept.[10] To fully understand the value of freedom, one must be able to imagine a life of nonfreedom. There were two distinctive social groups in Athens (aside from the differences between men and women): the free person and the slave. The Greek word for freedom was *eleutheria* which roughly translates to *not unfree* or *not a slave*.[11] A free person could move about, choose his occupation, have access to legal redress, and be allowed to speak freely; a slave lived a life of absolute domination. This idea of freedom as a social concept that distinguished a citizen from a slave was related to freedom as a geopolitical concept. A polis was free if it was not dominated or enslaved by foreigners.[12]

Athens was the birthplace of a vibrant and fluid style of government that required citizen participation. Native-born, land-owning male citizens gathered to decide all current matters according to majority vote. There was no superior authority and the citizens ruled themselves directly without entrusting their political voice to representatives. Meetings of the citizenry were frequent and previously agreed upon policies could be easily modified or abandoned. Certain powers were necessarily delegated, such as military leader or foreign ambassador, but these officials served for only one year and were reelected or replaced according to the will of the people.

Pericles was an Athenian politician who emphasized the importance of the moral and social basis of politics. His funeral oration was so well-known by the founding generation that many could recite it from memory. His theme was the Athenian citizens who were made great by what they valued. Although he was certainly engaging in some hyperbole with the flowery rhetoric expected in a funeral oration, Pericles claimed that Athenians valued equality, self-sufficiency, personal autonomy, recognition of merit above social status, respect for the laws, and most importantly, the "courage to be free."[13] He suggested that freedom of speech was the reason why Athenians were so wise and successful. "Our strength lies . . . not in deliberation and discussion," spoke Pericles, "but that knowledge which is gained by discussion preparatory to action. For we have a peculiar power of thinking before we act, and of acting, too, whereas other men are courageous from ignorance but hesitate upon reflection."[14]

Although the emphasis that was placed on freedom in the foundation of America may be traced to Athens, it should be stressed that the eighteenth-century ideas about personal and political liberty were quite different. Although the concept of *arete*, the idea of living up to one's individual fulfillment, was important in many of the Greek myths, the Athenians had little understanding of autonomous freedom as an immutable political right. Despite the relative freedom of movement and speech that was glorified by Pericles, in Athens there was no concept of an individual right to non-interference by the community. Responsibility to the polis was the key to understanding their conception of freedom. All citizens were required to participate in government and to join the military during times of war. If a citizen was willing to vote for war, he had to be willing to fight in that war—regardless of how inconvenient that may have been. With no requirement for a specific law to have been violated, anyone could be sent into exile (ostracized) by a majority vote of his fellow citizens for nothing more serious than for just being an annoyance. Socrates was sentenced to death for the vague charge of corrupting the youth and worshiping foreign gods. He in turn argued that as a citizen it was his duty to abide by the decision, even though he disagreed with it.

Not only were Athenians untroubled by the institution of slavery, they had no problem with depriving foreigners of freedom as they expanded their empire. Freedom was not a universal value. They believed that during the Greco-Persian wars of 499–449 BC, the Persians were beaten because the Athenians enjoyed freedom and the Persians were slavish barbarians. Their greater autonomy in conducting their own affairs was what had allowed them to defeat a much larger army.[15] According to Herodotus, the reason why freedom was a good thing was that it led to the collective greatness of Athens. When ruled by tyrants the Athenians "were not a whit more valiant than any of their neighbors . . . they let themselves be beaten, since then they worked for a master."[16]

The level of political engagement by citizens that was the cornerstone of Athenian democracy was rejected by the founders who saw it as impracticable and undesirable. History had demonstrated that democracy would collapse into tyranny because the people could be too easily manipulated by errant leaders. The founders' vision of political liberty existed on the continuum between what was theoretically practiced in Athens and what was advocated by Plato. Plato's vision of a well-run state was that government should be run by the capable and qualified. "The natural thing is for the sick person, rich or poor, to knock at the doctor's door," Plato explained, "and for anyone who needs to be ruled to knock at the door of the one who can rule him."[17] The idealization of personal freedom, however, that was expressed by Pericles continued to resonate. Personal freedom, as opposed to unjustified or excessive tyranny from others, was invigorating to the soul and allowed for the greatest human flourishing. The more direct source for the founders' vision of political liberty was indisputably Rome.[18]

ROMAN LIBERATAS

"There is no good government but what is Republican," wrote Adams in his influential pamphlet, *Thoughts on Government*.[19] This was not only due to Rome's importance in the ancient world, but resulted from the founders reading of their favorite ancient Roman writers such as Cicero, Sallust, Tacitus, and (the originally Greek) Plutarch. These writers from the later period of the Empire compared the political corruption and social sickness they were experiencing with an imagined former time of an idealized republic. They explained how the social and political structures of the early Roman republic had promoted virtue, happiness, and stability. Those idyllic early years had been ruined. Irresponsible and incompetent oligarchs, extreme inequalities in wealth, the growth of factions concerned only with short-term benefits and no common purpose, and the feckless people voting for anyone who made the best promises were just a few of the causes that, according to the wistful recorders of the glorious past, had led to the collapse of the republic.

Roman liberty was born around 500 BC with the expulsion of the last king by Brutus, the early leader of the republic. The Roman political principle of consent rather than coercion was symbolized in the idealization of the goddess Liberty.[20] As it had in Athens, the existence of slavery clarified to the concept of personal liberty. To be free meant that one was not a slave: they were free of total subjection by another.[21] The wearing of the iconic white toga, in fact, was what distinguished the free citizen from the slave. Freedom included a variety of privileges such as the right to choose an occupation or marriage partner, but just as with the Athenians, it was never thought to be a universal or unalienable right. Few other than the Roman people were believed to be capable or deserving of liberty.[22] Nor did the Roman idea of liberty include the idea of significant autonomy or non-interference by the community. Historians debate the significance or influence of sumptuary laws in ancient Rome, nonetheless, the fact of the existence of legal efforts at limiting personal choices — particularly when deemed hurtful to the community — would indicate an acceptance of limits to free choice.[23] Roman citizens were expected to participate in religious pageants, and there were no guarantees of free speech.[24]

What constituted political liberty for the Roman people was not direct participation, but the sovereignty that was placed in the people as a whole. Freedom meant that one was governed by laws that one participated in establishing and enforcing. From the Romans, the founders inherited the idea of a balanced constitution that contained a mixture of democracy, aristocracy, and monarchy. Government required a broad base of support from the mass of the people, but it should be controlled by those most capable of handling power, and it required a strong leader to execute the laws. The center of power was in a senate that was composed of aristocrats and former magistrates. The assemblies were made up of the citizens of Rome who elected the consuls. The consuls were the highest elected political officers who served important judiciary and military functions. Whether the wealthy influenced the voters through outright patronage or subtler methods of persuasion can be debated, the fact remained that the Roman Republic was oligarchic with the voice of the great mass of citizens somewhat limited.[25]

The way the Roman republic actually functioned was chaotic. For the founders, there were two transcendent messages concerning political liberty that rose above the discordant history. First, it was the best way to structure government. Balanced government was the ideal. When the republic was properly functioning the powers of the consuls (monarchy), the senate (aristocracy), and the plebeian assemblies (democracy) were balanced. Cicero wrote, when a single monarch ruled, "no one else has sufficient access to shared justice or to deliberative responsibility;" with aristocracies "the people have hardly any share in liberty;" and since degrees of status must be recognized, rule by the people would not be acceptable.[26]

The second lesson was that all liberty was ultimately founded on a concept of justice based in equality before the law—and ultimately on a belief in the existence of natural law. All laws must be built on the bedrock of morality. "True law is right reason," wrote Cicero, "consonant with nature, spread through all people. . . . It is wrong to pass laws obviating this law; it is not permitted to abrogate any of it; it cannot be and the person who does not obey it will be in exile from himself."[27]

Athenian prosperity was built on slavery and the Roman republic was dominated by the wealthy; these ancient models were nonetheless important to the founders. They provided historic framework for expressing the importance of liberty. The day-to-day details and the many fluctuations in how these governments functioned was not as important as what they symbolized: an exaltation of liberty. Their use of the ancient models was imprecise, the details frequently blurred, and much of their histories had been refracted and refined, but the underlying message was unmistakable. Citizenship in a correctly functioning state meant freedom. Freedom was fragile.

NOTES

1. John Adams, *A Defense of the Constitutions of Government of the United States of America* (London: 1787), 46.
2. "Research & Collections: Isaac H. Tiffany," Thomas Jefferson Monticello, accessed March 7, 2018, https://www.monticello.org/site/research-and-collections/isaac-h-tiffany.
3. Alexander Hamilton, "No. 9," in *The Federalist Papers : The Gideon Edition*, ed. James McClellan and George W. Carey, Gideon ed. (Indianapolis: Liberty Fund, 2001), 37.
4. James Madison, "No. 14," George W. Carey and James McClellan, eds., *The Federalist: By Alexander Hamilton, John Jay and James Madison*, Gideon ed. (Indianapolis: Liberty Fund, 2001), 67.
5. Gordon S. Wood, *The Creation of the American Republic, 1776–1787* (Chapel Hill: Published for the Institute of Early American History and Culture at Williamsburg, VA, by the University of North Carolina Press, 1969), 52.
6. The neoclassical architecture in the nation's capital was meant to evoke the principles that guided the founders. There is some inconsistency here in that the great majority of the surviving buildings were constructed during the period of the Roman Empire and not the Republic.
7. Thomas L. Pangle, "Republicanism and Rights," in *The Framers and Fundamental Rights*, ed. Robert A. Licht (Washington, DC: AEI Press, 1991), 7–8.
8. David Schmidtz and Jason Brennan, *A Brief History of Liberty* (Chichester, UK: Wiley-Blackwell, 2010), 43.
9. Plutarch, "Solon," in *Plutarch's Lives*, ed. Arthur Hugh Clough (New York: The Modern Library, 2001), I: 116.
10. The American revolutionaries commonly used the rhetoric of slavery when they spoke of their relationship with England. Leading up to the Civil War, Southerners (ironically) also spoke of their fear of being enslaved by the North.
11. Ibid., 19. Also see Quentin Skinner, *Liberty Before Liberalism* (Cambridge: Cambridge University Press, 1998), 37–48.
12. Richard Mulgan, "Liberty in Ancient Greece," in *Conceptions of Liberty in Political Philosophy*, ed. Zbigniew Pelczynski and John Gray (London: Athlone Press, 1984), 9.
13. Thucydides, "Pericles' Funeral Oration," University of Minnesota Human Rights Library, accessed January 5, 2018, http://hrlibrary.umn.edu/education/thucydides.html.
14. Kurt Raaflaub, *The Discovery of Freedom in Ancient Greece*, trans. Renate Franciscono (Chicago: University of Chicago Press, 2004), 250.
15. Schmidtz and Brennan, *A Brief History of Liberty*, 46.
16. Herodotus, "The History of Herodotus Book V," trans. George Rawlinson, The Internet Classics Archive, accessed March 18, 2018, http://classics.mit.edu/Herodotus/history.5.v.html.
17. Plato, "Republic VI," in *Plato: Complete Works*, 1112.
18. Gordon S. Wood, *The Creation of the American Republic: 1776–1787* (Chapel Hill: Univ. of North Carolina Press, 1998), 49.
19. John Adams, "Thoughts on Government (April 1776)," The Adams Papers Digital Editions, accessed January 19, 2018, https://www.masshist.org/publications/apde2/view?&id=PJA04dg2.
20. J. Rufus Fears, "Antiquity: The Example of Rome," in *An Uncertain Legacy: Essays on the Pursuit of Liberty*, ed. Edward B. McLean (Wilmington, DE: Intercollegiate Studies Institute, 1997), 3.
21. Raaflaub, *The Discovery of Freedom in Ancient Greece*, 267.
22. Fears, "Antiquity," 10.
23. See Valentina Arena, "Roman sumptuary legislation: Three concepts of liberty," *European Journal of Political Theory* 10, no. 4 (2011)
24. Fears, "Antiquity," 11.

25. A. Yakobson, "Traditional Political Culture and the People's Role in the Roman Republic," *Historia : Zeitschrift Für Alte Geschichte* 59, no. 3 (2010): 1–2, accessed January 9, 2018, http://proxy.library.georgetown.edu/login?url=https://search.proquest.com/docview/746422617?accountid=11091.

26. Cicero, *On the Commonwealth*, 1.43.

27. Ibid., 3.33.

FIVE
Two Paths to Virtue

Religion and Reason

The American idea of liberty is an amalgam of the philosophy of John Locke; Christianity, particularly the beliefs of New England Calvinists; and Deism, the religion of the Enlightenment, with its insistence that the only route to truth was rational thought. The Athenians and Romans held that freedom came from the laws and was fulfilled within the community. The veneration of the individual citizen had not been a significant concept in the politics of the ancient world. Yet one of the most important facets of the founders' understanding of liberty was the belief in an unalienable right to individual choice. Good choices, however, were built from a sound foundation of morality. When Jesus said "the truth will set you free" he was referring to this higher form of knowledge that was the basis for true freedom. One must first choose to be good before one could choose to be free. Submission to an ethical code was fundamental to the founders' concept of freedom.

The first section of this chapter will challenge the Lockean over-emphasis on autonomous self-interest that has dominated modern interpretations of liberty. One of the reasons why the modern ideas about liberty have gone astray is due to the excessive prominence that is placed today on the philosophy of liberal individualism.[1] Consistent with Christian principles that were dominant in the American colonies, there was a moral depth with an emphasis on human connectedness that was central to the founders' worldview. True freedom did not come from the laws of man; it resulted from personal choices to abide by an ethical system that came from God. Placing community interests before the self—public good liberty—had been a principal value to the ancients, and Christian teachings underscored the importance of communal well-being. As the

Jewish scholar Hillel wrote two-thousand years ago, the single most important message of what would become Judeo-Christian morality was to love thy neighbor, the rest was commentary.

CHRISTIANITY AND DEISM

Christianity was an important line of lineage that contributed to the eighteenth-century understanding of how America was supposed to function. We have been reminded of this throughout US history as numerous political movements have woven Christianity into their agendas and rhetoric. Both the Populist and Progressive movements of the late nineteenth and early twentieth centuries worked Christian images into their ideologies. Addressing the monetary issues of the day, William Jennings Bryan mesmerized his audiences with rhetorical references to a "crown of thorns" and accusations that the powerful eastern bankers were crucifying "mankind upon a cross of gold." The Progressives popularized the question "what would Jesus do?" In the late twentieth-century Christianity was appropriated by the evangelical right wing of the Republican party. From the other end of the political spectrum, liberation theology has taken a Marxist orientation to Christianity. Each of these political movements held that revitalized Christian principles of morality and community would cure the disorders that were threatening the nation's well-being.

The religious attachments of particular founders and the degree to which they were directly influenced by those affiliations has been the subject of much scholarly attention.[2] Whether it was Calvinism or any of the other Protestant sects that flourished in America, it is beyond dispute that Christianity was important in eighteenth-century America and it helped shape revolutionary thinking. Professor Donald Lutz, for example, looked at over three thousand of the citations in a wide range of the writings of the revolutionary generation. He found that a full 34 percent were from the Bible.[3]

Christianity emphasized the importance of the community and social responsibility. True freedom was not a private experience but could only occur with an understanding of our connections to others. This was a central religious truth that connected religion to policy, for even "wall of separation" Jefferson believed that the most important message from Jesus was to love our neighbors and to promote social harmony.[4] Jefferson wrote that the teachings of the ancient philosophers "related chiefly to ourselves, and the government of those passions which, unrestrained, would disturb our tranquility of mind. In this branch of philosophy, they were really great." However, Jefferson continued, "in developing our duties to others, they were short and defective." It was in the teachings of Jesus where "a system of morals is presented to us . . . the most perfect and sublime that has ever been taught by man." In his summary of Jesus's message, Jefferson articulated the essence of public good liberty. "His moral doctrines, relating to kindred and friends, were more pure and perfect than those of the most correct of the philosophers," wrote Jefferson. Jesus taught "a universal philanthropy, not only to kindred and friends, to neighbors and countrymen; but to all mankind, gathering all into one family, under the bonds of love, charity, peace, and common wants and common aids."[5]

That the Puritan settlers of New England viewed their liberty as a collective condition can be seen in just about any of the documents that have survived from the earliest years of settlement. They were the earliest notes of liberty that would resonate through American history. In the first recorded sermon delivered at Plymouth in 1621, Robert Cushman preached to the settlers that social bondedness was required if they were to prevail. A man who does not acknowledge his social connectedness was living as "a beast in the shape of a man." Cushman wrote (English is modernized in all of the following quotes):

> Now brethren, I pray you, remember yourselves, and know, that you are not in a retired monastical course, but have given your names and promises one to another and covenanted here to cleave together in the service of God, and the King; What then must you do? . . . you must seek still the wealth of one another; and enquire as David, how liveth such a man? How is he clad? How is he fed? . . . He is as good a man as I, and we are bound each to other . . . and his welfare my welfare, for I am as he is.[6]

This idea of living in a commonwealth where the welfare of others must take precedence over individualism in order to attain a higher level of human flourishing was the unmistakable theme in John Winthrop's famous 1630 sermon "A Model of Christian Charity" more commonly known as the "City upon a Hill" speech. The idea that togetherness was inextricably connected with the good life was the unmistakable theme:

> We must be knit together in this work as one man, we must entertain each other in brotherly Affection, we must be willing to abridge ourselves of our superfluities, for the supply of others necessities, we must uphold a familiar Commerce together in all meekness, gentleness, patience and liberality, we must delight in each other, make others Conditions our own rejoice together, mourn together, labor, and suffer together, always having before our eyes our Commission and Community in the work, our Community as members of the same body.[7]

The Mayflower Compact of 1620 is identified as the first written effort at creating a political community and offers insight into the settlers' original attempt at self-definition. Their intention was unambiguous: advance the Christian faith, and combine themselves into one body to make laws that were for the good of the community. The voyage was undertaken for the

"Glory of God, and Advancement of the Christian Faith, and the Honour of Our King and Country," and they promised to:

> covenant and combine ourselves together into a civil Body Politick, for our better Ordering and Preservation, and Furtherance of the Ends aforesaid: And by Virtue hereof do enact, constitute, and frame, such just and equal Laws, Ordinances, Acts, Constitutions, and Officers, from time to time, as shall be thought most meet and convenient for the general Good of the Colony; unto which we promise all due Submission and Obedience.[8]

In 1645 John Winthrop, the governor of the Massachusetts colony, delivered a speech that stressed the connections between liberty and Christianity. Liberty was the ability to resist evil, and Christian morality was the basis upon which citizens would tolerate authority. The lowest expression of liberty was for a man to simply do anything he wanted "it is a liberty to evil as well as to good . . . this liberty makes men grow more evil and in time to be worse than brute beasts." The highest expression of liberty was connected to the "covenant between God and man" and required that the civil authorities remained "good, just, and honest." Subjection to authority that was not operating according to principles of Christian justice was wrong and should be resisted. Proper authority "is of the same kind of liberty wherewith Christ hath made us free."[9]

In a sermon preached in 1757, true human freedom was inextricably connected with Christianity. Lovers of liberty must love the Christian religion for it "sets you at liberty from evil, and gives you a liberty to all that is good." The contrasting association of slavery with freedom, that had been important to the Greeks and Romans, was highlighted. Sin was slavery, for "all sinners are bonds-men and slaves, many persons are greatly mistaken, they do not know when they are slaves and when they are at liberty." These were the truths that seekers after freedom must understand:

> We must know this, that the freedom wherewith Christ had made us free, has nothing of licentiousness or lawless liberty in it; we must by no means imagine that it is a freedom from the obligation of the law of nature, and right reason; as it is a rule of obedience, none are born with a liberty to do what they will, neither has our Savior purchased any such liberty, for any to follow the dictates of their own mind.[10]

Jonathan Boucher was a prominent American clergymen and Loyalist who was eventually forced to flee the colonies in 1775 before the outbreak of the war. Although his beliefs led him to reject the move toward colonial independence, they were a clear expression of the Christian ideas that connected liberty to self-control and obedience to government that promoted morality. "True liberty," wrote Boucher, "is a liberty to do everything that is right, and being restrained from doing anything that is wrong." Boucher wrote that obedience was every man's duty because it is every man's interest; but it is particularly incumbent on Christians, because (in addition to its moral fitness) it is enjoined by the positive commands of God; and, therefore, when Christians are disobedient to human ordinances, they are also disobedient to God. If the form of government under which the good providence of God has been pleased to place us be mild and free, it is our duty to enjoy it with gratitude and with thankfulness and, in particular, to be careful not to abuse it by licentiousness.[11]

If there is one idea in this book that stands above all others, it is that the founders were united in the belief that, in the words of John Adams, "Religion and Morality alone [could] establish the Principles upon which Freedom can securely stand. . . . The foundation of a free Constitution, is pure Virtue."[12] This was an important lesson from antiquity that merged with the covenant theology of the New England Puritans. God granted man freedom, and man had the duty to be moral. Freedom and morality: one did not work without the other. The extent to which Americans believed that liberty was contingent upon religious moral teachings is poorly understood and is the aspect of liberty from which we have disconnected the most.

Deism was at the other end of the religious spectrum from New England Calvinism, but just as important. It was the religion of moral teachings, lifted above the trappings of organized religion with its accepted dogma, and subjected to the scrutiny of reason. The historian and professor of religious studies, Richard Holmes, concluded that many of the founders had accepted certain tenets of Deism. The first five presidents of the United States were Deist to one extent or another.[13] "Deism was a prevailing religious sentiment not only in parts of the United States," wrote Holmes, "In Virginia it was the dominant interpretation of religion among educated males."[14]

The freedom that the founders envisioned for America was based on a new vision of how people were intended to live. It logically followed that they would be drawn to a system of religious beliefs that promoted the original purity of what God wanted for mankind. The gift of reason was the instrument to uncover that mystery. Edward Herbert, identified as the founding father of Deism, questioned the traditional Christian beliefs concerning salvation and damnation. "I found that their opinion was grounded not on reason," wrote Herbert, "how could I believe that a just God could take pleasure in the eternal reprobation of those to whom he never afforded any means of salvation." Herbert could not understand "how they could call that God *most good and great* who created man only to damn them, without their knowledge, and against their will."[15] Herbert argued that the priests had contaminated the teachings of pure religious thought with "superstition and idolatry" that contributed to conflict and dissent. The answer was to find the basic universal truths that should guide religious behavior. Lining up with the Declaration's self-evident truths about basic rights that had come from the Creator, Herbert discovered basic truths that were common to all religions and were supported by reason. The truths were: (1) there was one God, (2) he ought to be worshiped, (3) virtue and piety are the most important parts of worship, (4) we should be sorry for our sins and repent, and (5) there will be rewards and punishments both in life and in death.[16]

Whether Calvinist or Deist, the message was clear: the good life was dependent on our efforts at virtuous living. People also choose to remain free by forming themselves into civil society. That was the essential point in Locke's theory and that was why the founders found his writings to be of particular usefulness when legitimizing their efforts at independence.

JOHN LOCKE

Locke wrote at a time of tremendous political turmoil in England. According to Locke, the revolution in England in 1688 that overthrew the king had been valid because the king had been abusive. Because governments were a human invention, when governments became abusive of the people it was the duty of the people to throw out the abusers and bring about new governments that would better protect their rightful liberty.

John Locke was not the first to have discussed natural law, compact government, or unalienable rights, yet he was one of the more influential of the Enlightenment philosophers for the American founders. According to Jefferson, the three greatest men to have ever lived were Locke, Francis Bacon, and Sir Isaac Newton.[17] Bacon told us to examine the evidence of experience. Newton proposed that the world was orderly and uniform. Locke taught that government was created by man in order to protect life, liberty, and property. The publication of Locke's *Two Treatises on Government* that immediately followed England's Glorious Revolution and the 1689 English Bill of Rights, assured that this British philosopher would be widely read in America.

Some historians have objected to an overly simplified view that the founders' understanding of liberty was derived primarily from John Locke. Donald Lutz pointed out, "it makes more sense to call Locke an American than it does to call America Lockean," for the American colonists were establishing governments based on what came to be called liberalism long before Locke published his treatises on government.[18] Undoubtedly, the earliest examples of contract government in the colonies emerged spontaneously in response to the immediate needs of the settlers. When it came to articulating the revolution against England, however, it was the writings of Locke whom they rephrased and summarized:

> The natural liberty of man is to be free from any superior power on earth and not to be under the will or legislative authority of man, but to have only the law of nature for his rule. The liberty of man, in society, is to be under no other legislative power, but that established by consent, in the commonwealth, nor under the dominion of any will, or restraint of any law, but what the legislative shall enact, according to the trust put in it.[19]

Scholars of the Declaration of Independence generally agree that Locke had the most direct influence on Jefferson's words. Richard Henry Lee's assertion that the Declaration was "copied from Locke's treatise on government"[20] may be a bit of hyperbole. Nonetheless, Jefferson's phraseology was very close, as the following comparison demonstrates. The first is an excerpt from Locke and the second from the Declaration

> Great mistakes in the ruling part, many wrong and inconvenient laws, and all the slips of human frailty, will be borne by the people without mutiny or murmur. But if a long train of abuses, prevarications and artifices, all tending the same way, make the design visible to the people, and they cannot but feel what they lie under.[21]

> But when a long train of abuses and usurpations, pursuing invariably the same Object evinces a design to reduce them under absolute Despotism, it is their right, it is their duty, to throw off such Government, and to provide new Guards for their future security.

According to Locke, natural law was God's truth. Locke believed that natural law could be discovered through the activation of our human capacity to reason; hence the doctrine of self-evidence. Our God-given powers of reason, if properly engaged, would enlighten mankind to the laws of nature and the appropriate behaviors that lead to true happiness. In Locke's hypothetical original state of nature, all were "equal and independent" members of one universal community; and "no one ought to harm another in his life, health, liberty, or possessions."[22] Yet the experience of liberty in this natural state had its drawbacks. Some men can become degenerate and noxious, conflicts would arise over resources, and the weak would be dominated by those few individuals who chose to violate God's law. To protect freedom violators must be punished. In the state of nature, the punishment that an injured party imposed upon an offender, though justified by the right of self-preservation, might not be reasonable and proportionate. An important barrier to tyranny is the belief that no one person can be judge, jury, and executioner for their own cause. To prevent this from happening, men form a civil society where they work out reasonable rules concerning acceptable behaviors and punishments. Civil society ensured greater peace and safety. Natural law was antecedent to civil law, yet civil law could not totally overcome natural law in that natural law could never be violated. Civil law existed in order to protect natural freedom; it could not prohibit the freedom that natural law allowed.

Locke's twofold theory of liberty concerned both personal and political liberty. The people instituted governments that allowed for a sphere of protection for the individual, or as Jefferson wrote when he summarized Locke in the Declaration, "organizing its powers in such form, as to them shall seem most likely to effect their Safety and Happiness." In Locke's ontology, humans lived independently and it was self-interest that motivated the creation of political communities. Individualism was first; the political community was second. American romanticizing of the rugged individual was influenced by Locke and accentuates the importance of personal liberty. This idea that was introduced by Hobbes, who had concluded that only an all-powerful central authority could govern, was softened by Locke who concluded that humans were not so completely antagonistic and could participate in self-government.

Locke's theories about political and personal liberty have significant connections to the importance of the concept of internal liberty that is integral to this project. The condition of freedom in nature was not to be under the will of another, yet this freedom was not an absolute license to do whatever. One was not free if he or she was under the influence of irrational wants or unchecked passions. People needed internalized self-set limits so they would not violate the laws of nature and harm themselves or their neighbors. Locke's reasoning in this regard is connected to the premises concerning human nature that come from Aristotle and Christianity.[23] Locke's theories are based on an Aristotelian view of human nature in that liberty and the hoped-for human flourishing could only be accomplished through reason:

> The *freedom* then of man, and liberty of acting according to his own will, is *grounded* on his having *reason*, which is able to instruct him in that law he is to govern himself by, and make him know how far he is left to the freedom of his own will. To turn him loose to an unrestrained liberty, before he has reason to guide him, is not the allowing him the privilege of his nature to be free; but to thrust him out amongst brutes, and abandon him to a state as wretched, and as much beneath that of a man, as theirs.[24]

Rational thought is employed not only to discover the best way to live, but also to discover God's truth concerning our moral obligations. "For men being all the workmanship of one omnipotent, and infinitely wise maker;" wrote Locke, "all the servants of one sovereign master, sent into the world by his order, and about his business; they are his property, whose workmanship they are, made to last during his, not one another's pleasure."[25] Locke suggested that if more people operated with internal restraints, then fewer external restraints would be necessary. This idea of internal liberty, or the practice of enlightened virtuous living, was the essential factor to the great experiment in liberty that the founders were undertaking.

The founders were armed with the historic evidence that liberty was the foundation of human flourishing. From the Ancient Greeks and Romans, the founders learned that the best protection of liberty was to be found in a government where sovereignty rested with the people. It is important to remember that in both Greece and Rome slaves made up a very high percentage of the population. Given that women, foreigners, and slaves had no political power, these states were actually ruled by a relatively small group of elites. The importance of individual freedom and of the existence of a natural equality came from Christianity and was expanded upon by the Enlightenment.

The founders also knew that all governments that had honored liberty had collapsed due to social changes, political factions, and had been ultimately corrupted by wealth and the love of luxury. Could Americans handle liberty? Were they virtuous enough? These questions were central to the colonial debates preceding the revolution. Gordon Wood wrote that these questions about "the kind of people Americans were and wanted to be" were more important than the specific economic or political questions. Americans believed that "on the one hand, they seemed to be particularly virtuous people, and thus unusually suited for republican government" and yet they worried over the potential for luxury and corruption that would undermine the republic.[26] Thomas Paine warned that "virtue . . . is not hereditary, neither is it perpetual."[27] In the next chapter I will move from the abstract to the personal with a close-up examination of two founders and their struggles to "stay the course" toward the good life.

NOTES

1. See for example Barry Alan Shain, *The Myth of American Individualism: The Protestant Origins of American Political Thought* (Princeton, NJ: Princeton University Press, 1994), xiv.

2. Many of the founders such as Patrick Henry and Samuel Adams expressed traditional Christian beliefs. Thomas Jefferson was a Deist who denied the divinity of Christ or the miracles that were recorded in the Bible; he believed however, in the moral teachings of Jesus. See David Lynn Holmes, *The Religion of the Founding Fathers* (New York: Oxford University Press, 2006).

3. Michael Novak, *On Two Wings: Humble Faith and Common Sense at the American Founding* (San Francisco, CA: Encounter Books, 2002), 6.

4. Gordon S. Wood, *Revolutionary Characters: What Made the Founders Different* (New York: Penguin Books, 2007), 107.

5. Thomas Jefferson, "Jefferson to Doctor Benjamin Rush, 21 April 1803," *The Portable Thomas Jefferson*, ed. Merrill D. Peterson (Harmondsworth, UK: Penguin Books, 1977), 492

6. Robert Cushman, "The Sin and Danger of Self-Love Described by a Sermon Preached at Plymouth, in New-England, 1621," last modified October 30, 2013, accessed August 12, 2015, http://www.gutenberg.org/files/44071/44071-h/44071-h.htm.

7. John Winthrop, "A Model of Christian Charity," Digital History, accessed March 3, 2018, http://www.digitalhistory.uh.edu/disp_textbook.cfm?smtID=3&psid=3918.

8. "Mayflower Compact, 1620," The Avalon Project: Documents in Law, History, and Diplomacy, accessed March 18, 2018, http://avalon.law.yale.edu/17th_century/mayflower.asp.

9. John Winthrop, "On Liberty (1645)," Constitution Society, accessed February 3, 2018, http://www.constitution.org/bcp/winthlib.htm.

10. Joshua Tufts, "The believers most sure freedom purchased by Jesus Christ, laid down in a sermon preached at Narragansett, No 1. 1757. By Joshua Tufts, A.M. preacher of the Gospel there. Published at the desire of the hearers.," Early American Imprints, accessed February 2, 2018, http://0-infoweb.newsbank.com.gull.georgetown.edu/iw-search/we/Evans?p_theme=eai&p_product=EAIX&d_collections=EVAN&d_collectionName=EVAN&p_action=doc&p_topdoc=1&p_docnum=1&d_searchform=customized&p_text_custbase-0=8051&p_field_custbase-0=docnum&p_sort=YMD_date:D&p_nbid=M43U43WAMTUxNzU5NDczMy4yNDQwNzg6MToxMzoxNDEuMTYxLjM4LjQ1&p_docref=.

11. Jonathan Boucher, "On Civil Liberty, Passive Obedience, and Nonresistance," Constitution Society, accessed February 3, 2018, http://www.constitution.org/bcp/nonresis.htm.

12. "John Adams to Zabdiel Adams, 21 June 1776," *Founders Online*, National Archives, version of January 18, 2019, https://founders.archives.gov/documents/Adams/04-02-02-0011.

13. David Lynn Holmes, *The Religion of the Founding Fathers* (New York: Oxford University Press, 2006), 109.

14. Ibid., 164.

15. Edward Herbert, "The Antient Religion of the Gentiles, and Causes of Their Errors Consider'd: The Mistakes and . . .," trans. William Lewis, Internet Archive, last modified January 15, 2008, accessed January 21, 2020, https://archive.org/details/antientreligion00chergoog.

16. Ibid.

17. "Thomas Jefferson to Benjamin Rush, 16 January 1811," *Founders Online*, National Archives, version of January 18, 2019, https://founders.archives.gov/documents/Jefferson/03-03-02-0231.

18. Ibid., 11.

19. John Locke, Chapter IV "Of Slavery," (section 22) in *Second Treatise of Government*, ed. C. B. MacPherson (Indianapolis: Hackett Publishing, 1980), 17.

20. Thomas Jefferson, "To James Madison from Thomas Jefferson, 30 August 1823," *Founders Online*, last modified November 26, 2017, accessed March 7, 2018, http://founders.archives.gov/documents/Madison/04-03-02-0113.

21. Locke, Chapter XIX "On the Dissolution of Government," (section 225) in *Second Treatise*, 113.

22. Locke, Chapter II "On the State of Nature," (section 6) in *Second Treatise*, 9.

23. James Tully, "Locke on Liberty," in *Conceptions of Liberty in Political Philosophy*, ed. Zbigniew Pelczynski and John Gray (London: Athlone Press, 1984), 65.

24. Locke, Chapter II "On the State of Nature," (section 63) in *Second Treatise*, 35.

25. Ibid., (section 6) in *Second Treatise*, 9.

26. Wood, *The Creation of the American Republic*, 93.

27. Quoted in Wood, *The Creation of the American Republic*, 65.

SIX

Benjamin Franklin and Thomas Jefferson

The Art of Moderation

Chapter 3 examined how moderation was a central pillar to building the good life. Aristotle, Epicurus, and Cicero taught that the primary activity for the fulfilled life was to sustain a constancy of purpose in searching for the middle point between behavioral extremes. This model of moderation that was inherited from the philosophers of antiquity merged with Enlightenment thinking. A portrait of the temperate and self-controlled individual emerged as the ego-ideal for the founders' generation. "The spirit of moderation should be that of the legislator, the political good, like the moral good, is always found between two limits,"[1] wrote Montesquieu, one of the most influential of the eighteenth-century philosophers. A wise person would understand that the good life was guided by internalizing well-understood standards of virtuous conduct. Navigating the middle course was the route to discovering this state of virtue. To live a life of moderation, to be reasonable, modest, sensible, judicious, restrained—all synonyms for moderation—was the vital characteristic for the successful life. One must wonder, however, about our founders' psychological integration.

They were revolutionaries. In our current excess glorifying era, the idea of moderation more readily brings to mind an image of a conservative fence-straddler. Engaging in a revolution against the mother-of-all-mother countries, attempting to separate a colony from the empire—something that had never happened before—and establish a new nation based on radical (for the day) liberty, would certainly be the work of throw-caution-to-the wind, fire-breathing extremists. Indeed, the founders never claimed to be modest men, for diffident men do not become bold revolutionary leaders. They believed that a natural aristocracy existed among men and that the gifted elite should rise above the rabble to lead. The aging Jefferson wrote to Adams in 1813 concerning the commonly held opinion that, "there is a natural aristocracy among men."[2] One of the most important reasons for why the founders preferred a representative republic over a democracy was that the former would be more likely to lift the "natural aristoi into the offices of government."[3]

How did this work? How did a generation fight for ideas that were the most radical for their time, be willing to risk their lives and everything they held dear, yet be considered men of moderation? The answer circles back to the metaphor of a four-note musical chord that is at the core of this project: the founders' understanding of liberty involved an equilibrium among four important conditions. Political and personal liberty, with all the potential for civic chaos and personal excess that those two activities may lead to (as history had taught), must be stabilized with the vigilant self-policing of internal liberty and a benevolent spirit of public good liberty. Since the American revolutionaries were determined to replace British rule with a form of limited government that would greatly expand political and personal liberty beyond traditional boundaries, an even greater moral fortitude would be required from the citizens.

This was essentially a battle against nature. Just as entropy in nature is a drive toward disorder, political systems with a balanced distribution of power were unstable. A concerted exertion of energy is required to slow this tendency. To resist the slide into political disorder, it was supremely important that the citizens be prepared to exert the effort to self-regulate. Corrupt government was the end result of a people having lost their ethical moorings. Moral strength, especially among the leadership, would be crucial in order to resist the consolidation of power to which liberty had always fallen victim. Only a virtuous people could conduct public affairs in an orderly manner. In no place was this as important as in America, where a relatively egalitarian context with no entrenched aristocracy would allow for men from a variety of backgrounds to achieve political prominence. Alexis de Tocqueville addressed the importance of character for men who achieved status in a socially fluid society when he wrote "what is to be feared, moreover, is not so much the sight of the immorality of the great as that of immorality leading to greatness."[4]

The founders believed that if citizens sustained a constancy of effort at good character, American liberty would survive. In the preceding chapters I have taken a broad look at the historical panorama. In this chapter I will move from the abstract to the personal and take a closer look at two of the founders—Benjamin Franklin and Thomas Jefferson—to see how they managed the problem of moderating their own behavior. They were far from perfect role models. The fact that their lofty words did not always match their behavior does not mean they should be dismissed as hypocrites. They were human. They did not always live up to their ideals, but at least they tried to reach them.

An autobiography written by Franklin and a twelve-page letter written by Jefferson will be the two primary sources. In writing an autobiography an author essentially becomes two people separated by time; one is the protagonist of the story and the other is the judge. Franklin constructed his narrative around the leitmotif of his personal failings and his efforts at taking control of his life through rigorous efforts at moderating his behavior and becoming a more virtuous and orderly person. To find first-hand evidence of Jefferson's internal struggles with psychological moderation presented more of a challenge. Jefferson was not one to let his feelings show.[5] A letter written to Jefferson's love interest Maria Cosway, the only love letter in the massive collection of Jefferson's correspondences,[6] has been identified by historians as a portal through which we might glimpse his efforts toward mental orderliness that makes the virtuous life possible. Here as well we will see Jefferson as the actor and the judge as he struggled to moderate his behavior and uphold a balanced ideal.

Case studies from two men of such different backgrounds and who achieved positions of great power demonstrate that the character issue was a broad reaching concern for the founders and not just idiosyncratic to one generation or demographic. One came from a position of privilege, the other from a hard-scrabble childhood. Although both are grouped in the collective we call the Founding Fathers, they were from different generations, with Franklin old enough to have been Jefferson's father. Jefferson was the oldest son from a prominent "First Family of Virginia," who benefitted from early contact with some of the most distinguished colonial scholars while a student at William and Mary. "From his earliest memories his financial position was assured," wrote Jefferson's Pulitzer Prize winning biographer Dumas Malone, "and the best educational opportunities which the Colony afforded were later available to him."[7]

Franklin, from poor New England immigrant stock, was the youngest son of a youngest son for five generations (the fifteenth child in a family of seventeen) and attended only two years of formal education. From this obscure beginning we come to the image of Franklin amiably bustling about Philadelphia or charming the regulars in the French salons with his "untroubled high spirits, his gaiety and wit, his social success, and above all his casual insouciance."[8] Franklin might be the most European of any of the founders, having lived for many years abroad, mixing easily with "lords and aristocrats in Britain and the rest of Europe. He conversed with kings and even dined with one."[9] The long-limbed and head-ache prone image of the introverted Jefferson is starkly different from the corpulent Franklin in every way. Jefferson was first and foremost a Virginian, feeling only fully at home on his mountain top refuge where he retreated when political life became too conflicted.[10] He is well known for his writing, but preferred not to speak in public (and he was not very good when he did.)[11]

When we look at these two, perhaps the most well-known champions of the American Revolution, we can see that each struggled with the need to moderate their private lives and live a life of virtue. Both Franklin and Jefferson dealt with challenges at different points in their lives that personally revealed this essential truth: good character must be cultivated and the tendency toward personal license must be moderated. Or as Aristotle so famously taught: we are what we continually do. Franklin and Jefferson's generation was preoccupied with the possibility that the new nation would collapse into either anarchy or autocracy. Success or failure would ultimately be based on two variables: (1) Could they create a system of government that would be designed in such a way that liberty destroying power in any one part of society would be moderated? (2) Would the citizens be virtuous enough to handle liberty?

The lessons from history would suggest a very low probability for a positive outcome. Nonetheless, Franklin and Jefferson devoted themselves to what must be the quintessential Enlightenment answer to both of those questions: yes. Improvement of the human condition was possible. On the macro level, government could be created that would protect liberty (not destroy it as it always had in the past). On the micro level, citizens must be devoted to self-improvement and be conscious of the potential for internal impulses that could steer a person off the path of immoderate, and therefore unvirtuous, behavior. Personal liberty was protected by understanding its boundaries and through a concerted effort to lead a disciplined and moderate life. Gordon Wood, the author of numerous books on the people and ideology of the Revolution, wrote that the founders were keenly aware that "it was not the force of arms which made the ancient republics great or which ultimately destroyed them. It was rather the character and spirit of their people. Frugality, industry, temperance, and simplicity—the rustic traits of the sturdy yeoman—were the stuff that made a society strong."[12]

For Franklin, who did not write any formal political treatises, I will explore his *Autobiography* for access to his thoughts about the importance of virtue in human nature. The plan is to look at examples from his life where he was taking on the struggle of immoderate behavior. The *Autobiography* can be a puzzling source to work with. Franklin's writing style was charmingly humorous and at times quite revealing. On the other hand, as Wood described, "he always seems to be holding back . . . reticent, detached, not wholly committed" and scholars disagree over what Franklin was trying to accomplish in his autobiography.[13] Franklin's biographers tend to agree that he wore many masks.[14] Works on Franklin typically begin with a statement concerning the trouble with ever knowing who the real Franklin was.[15] Nonetheless, as a man who may have had "the fullest and deepest understanding of human nature"[16] of any of the founders, Franklin will be accepted as he endeavored to present himself. He was a truth-seeker and was not just posturing for admirers. It was through his personal account that Franklin intended to present his views on everything that mattered, from religion and morality to politics and modern technology.

Franklin's autobiography intertwined a description of his extraordinary achievements with a personal story of a flawed person, making mistakes, and struggling with self-improvement. The same cannot be said for Jefferson's brief autobiography. Jefferson is more enigmatic for he was reticent about his personal life.[17] His autobiography reads more like a narrative history than a personal memoir. There was no mention of personal scrapes—Franklin's errata—or struggles with how to build a virtuous life. "Biographers have always found Jefferson's private life a puzzle," wrote Richard Bernstein the author of numerous books and articles on Jefferson "in large measure because he carefully cloaked his inmost thoughts and feelings."[18] "Elusive, reserved, aloof" are the words most often used to describe him.[19] Jefferson saved copies of all the letters he wrote, yet he chose not to preserve the letters to his wife, the one he may have been the most willing to reveal his innermost thoughts. There was one letter, however, that provides a glimpse into Jefferson's personal struggles: the famous letter to Maria Cosway written as a dialogue between his head and his heart.

I cannot claim that this chapter will expose the real Franklin and Jefferson. "The reputations of those who the shape the fate of nations," wrote Bernard Bailyn, "are twisted and turned to fit the needs of those who follow, until, it seems, there is no such actual person left."[20] Indeed, Franklin and Jefferson have been both revered and disparaged according to changing political or social agendas. Jefferson's reputation, more so than Franklin's, has endured more highs and lows than any of the other founders. The "hysteria of denunciation" and the "hysteria of exaltation" began during his lifetime.[21] There are many reasons for the roller coaster ride of Jefferson's reputation; undoubtedly, he has become "the mirror in which each generation finds reflected its most urgent moral and political concerns."[22]

The choice of Jefferson should not require any further explanation, but perhaps a bit of clarification is required for why Franklin was chosen as opposed to any of the far more scholarly founders such as John Adams, John Dickinson, or James Wilson. Although Jefferson claimed that George Washington and Benjamin Franklin stood together as the two greatest heroes of the Revolution, Franklin's persona may seem to lack a certain gravitas when juxtaposed with the others. Since Jefferson wrote those words, the images of Washington and Franklin have diverged in the ongoing construction of their identities. The tendency has been to dismiss Franklin as morally shallow and self-serving.[23] Washington was the archetypal leader; the mythologized Cincinnatus. He has remained the severe and remote commanding general and president, with a personality as impervious as the Jean-Antoine Houdon statue or as one-dimensional as the Gilbert Stuart portrait.

Franklin's story has been more complex in the way that he has been both diminished and glorified; and his appearance shifts depending on perspective.[24] He was the charmingly quaint, kite-flying, racoon hat wearing writer of humorously witty sayings. He was the quintessential rags-to-riches American success story. He was one of the most lauded and brilliant Enlightenment scientists and inventors in the colonies. Although clearly a master of self-promotion and one of the more popular authors of his generation, his complex and poorly recorded diplomatic efforts during the Revolution cannot be easily summed up in a simplified and easily understood label such as "Father of Our Country," or "Author of the Declaration of Independence."[25]

Jefferson and Franklin also present to this writer a delightful sort of odd-couple earthy/ethereal polarity in everything from their physicality to their personas as history has transmitted them to the popular audience. Franklin never wore "his brains on his sleeve"[26] and his best-known contributions are the *Poor Richard's* aphorisms where he appealed to his reader as down-to-earth and at ease with the everyday predicaments of life. For this reason perhaps, Franklin's reputation as a deep thinker has been attacked by historians and other members of the intellectual elite.[27] This is in stark contrast with Jefferson's forceful summary of the Enlightenment in the Declaration that has ensconced him as a man of unfathomable brilliance.

John Adams had grumpily fretted about the future construction and consumption of history, and that Franklin's contributions to the Revolution would be disingenuously magnified:[28]

> The History of our Revolution will be one continued Lye from one End to the other. The Essence of the whole will be that Dr. Franklins electrical Rod, Smote the Earth and out Spring General Washington. That Franklin electrified him with his Rod—and thence forward these two conducted all the Policy Negotiations Legislation and War.[29]

To the contrary, Franklin's multifaceted contributions to the success of the Revolution and the writing of the Constitution were largely simplified into a homey narrative for popular consumption in the earliest decades of the Republic, with most of the early attention focused on his work with electricity.[30] As the story of America was written through the remainder of the nineteenth century, with the need to imbue it with patriotic messages, Franklin fell victim to the myth making that was important to building a spirit of nationalism. Accordingly, his story of success and self-dependence—a man who took control of his own destiny— was crafted for the young and new immigrants. Franklin became "Exhibit

A" of the American spirit and a man worth emulating in every way. His story was a type of celebrity endorsement for the American way of life.[31] Franklin became a unifying metaphor for the nation and his story proved that in America, greatness can come from the most difficult and humblest beginnings. All that was required was a lot of pluck and a virtuous determination for self-betterment.[32]

FRANKLIN'S AUTOBIOGRAPHY

The essential message of Franklin's story was that the happiest fulfillment was to be discovered through the management of our messy impulses, the cultivation of virtue, and an engagement in public service. As he wrote in the opening paragraph of the *Autobiography*, he had led a life "with a considerable Share of Felicity" and posterity might like to know how this was accomplished.[33] His biography was divided into four parts. Part one, written along the lines of Cicero's *De Officiis*, began as a letter to his son. Part two was less biographical in the traditional sense and addressed his efforts at becoming a more virtuous person. In parts three and four, Franklin returned to a biographical narrative and described the events of his life after achieving financial success and retiring from the printing business. These last sections covered many of his inventions and projects that were intended to promote the public good. The tone in parts three and four was less intimate than the first as it focused not just on personal stories but on the important political events of the day. This summary therefore will focus on parts one and two where he explicitly addressed his efforts at assuming authentic responsibility for moral improvement and are directly connected to the current project concerning moderation in the pursuit of virtue.

The basic outline of his narrative in part one can be quickly sketched. Franklin reports that he was the socially and intellectually precocious son of poor yet upstanding parents. His father was a well-known man of sound judgment who was often "consulted by private Persons about their Affairs when any Difficulty occur'd, & frequently chosen an Arbitrator between contending parties."[34] Unable to pay for formal education, Franklin's father did his best to turn time at the crowded dinner table into an informal school room where the importance of virtuous living was inculcated. Franklin wrote that his father "lik'd to have as often as he could, some sensible Friend or Neighbour, to converse with . . . . which might tend to improve the Minds of his Children. By this means he turn'd our Attention to what was good, just, & prudent in the Conduct of Life."[35]

At the age of twelve Franklin was apprenticed as a printer to an older brother in Boston. Ongoing conflicts with his brother ultimately resulted in his moving to Philadelphia where he continued in the printing trade.

Franklin's pattern of rigorous efforts at self-improvement was established early. Painfully aware of his lack of formal education, he busied his non-work hours with reading, writing, and studying arithmetic, logic, and rhetoric.[36] To direct more funds for the purchase of books he reduced his living costs by temporarily becoming a vegetarian.

In Philadelphia, Franklin made some prestigious contacts. One of Franklin's admirers arranged for him to travel to London where he lived for two years. Returning to Philadelphia he was briefly employed as a store clerk but ultimately found his way back to the printing business at which he clearly excelled. Part one ends with a description of how Franklin along with a small group of friends established the first subscription library. This was the earliest example of Franklin's belief that self-betterment was best promoted within a community context and that the protection of liberty was inextricably tied to the promotion of the public good. In other words, there was not only a lack of tension between the personal and the public good, but also, they worked together. Additionally, the idea that the more intellectually gifted could through their efforts uplift the common man would be important to the success of our system of government. Franklin wrote,

> These libraries have improved the general Conversation of the Americans, made the common Tradesman & Farmers as intelligent as most Gentlemen from other Countries, and perhaps have contributed in some degree to the Stand so generally made throughout the Colonies in Defense of their Privileges[37]

Using a printer's term for a mistake that is later corrected—errata—Franklin interspersed his narrative with the discussion of important turning points in his life. Historians have determined that the discussion of the errata were added at a later point in time and all at one sitting.[38] Perhaps the younger Franklin who wrote part one for the benefit of his son did not think he needed to include an examination of the less admirable periods of his life. It was the older Franklin who may have shifted the purpose of the narrative. Rather than just a recitation of the facts of his life that he would like to have remembered by posterity, he focused on life lessons that were learned through personal disappointments when good character faltered. The underlying theme of all these struggles was the value he placed on virtue. He addressed five significant occurrences of troublesome behavior. These errata had wrought short-term advantages but were, in hindsight, deviations from his moral ideal and were important turning points in his long-term project of self-improvement. They were points in his life when his self-absorption eclipsed his sense of decency and fairness to others. To have presented his personal story as having turned on a series of mistakes that he was able to correct, was important to a people undertaking a revolutionary experiment in democratic government. "The great privilege of the Americans is not only to be more enlightened than others," wrote Alexis de Tocqueville in his perceptive analysis, "but also to have the ability to make mistakes that can be corrected."[39]

The first two errata related to Franklin's difficulties with establishing economic and professional independence. He took advantage of some difficulties his brother encountered with the local government and connived his release from his indenture contract. The other involved a sum of money that a family friend had entrusted him for safe-keeping. He improvidently used the money to support himself and his friends, then placed a large amount of the blame for this misappropriation of funds on the excessive drinking of one of them. During this time, he lived in a perpetual state of worry that the money would be recalled. Fortunately, the family friend did not ask for the money until Franklin was able to replace the pilfered funds (with interest) for an unpaid debt might have landed Franklin in prison and would have damaged his reputation and derailed his prospects.

Franklin's time in London account for the other three errata. The first two involved youthful blunders with women. Sidetracked by the distractions of life with his first great adventure across the Atlantic, he wrote only one cursory letter to a woman he had developed an attachment with (his future wife) to state he would not be returning to Philadelphia any time soon.[40] Youthful exuberance, as well as "being at this time under no Religious Restraints,"[41] led him to make an improper romantic overture to a friend's girlfriend. The final erratum was in a different category from the others but according to Franklin was the underlying cause for all of them. Problems with a domineering older brother, money management, and women were common problems for a young man; an indiscretion that involved the printing of a metaphysical treatise, not so much.

Franklin wrote *A Dissertation on Liberty & Necessity, Pleasure and Pain* while still holding to a radical interpretation of Deism that he had adopted around the age of fifteen.[42] In this pamphlet he argued that since God had created a universe based on his "infinite Wisdom, Goodness & Power" it followed that there was no such thing as evil and that "nothing could possibly be wrong in the World, & that Vice & Virtue were empty Distinctions."[43] He ultimately rejected this belief because he found them to be, quite simply, not useful (irrespective of whether or not they were true).[44] Franklin had committed his errata while under the influence of this "freethinking."[45] He admitted to a youthful error in his metaphysical argument and became convinced that "Truth, Sincerity & Integrity" were the most important practices for "the Felicity of Life."[46]

There is a pedagogical logic to the arrangement of part one and part two. Franklin knew that the *Autobiography* would be widely read and therefore wrote with the intention of teaching future generations about the connection between virtue and a happy life. His approach to persuasion took a variety of forms. In part one he followed his own advice about how information was best communicated. "I wish well meaning sensible Men would not lessen their Power of doing Good by a Positive assuming Manner that seldom fails to disgust," wrote Franklin, "it tends to create Opposition, and to defeat every one of those Purposes for which Speech was given. . . . *Men should be taught as if you taught them not.*"[47] His coverage of the mistakes he had made as a result of youthful shortsightedness or when he was still under the spell of misguided beliefs were presented as simple parables that would illustrate the larger moral message. This arrangement allowed him to appear humbly flawed and neither dogmatic nor didactic.

Part two takes a less subtle approach and directly addressed the need to educate the future generations of a "rising people"[48] It opened with two letters from friends that explained why he decided to resume writing the *Autobiography*. The friends encouraged him to share the incidents from his life that would be useful in promoting the "rules of prudence in ordinary affairs." Franklin's story would "explain many things that all men ought to have once explained to them, to give them a chance of becoming wise by foresight."[49] Only through the development of virtuous character would the future be sustainable. Franklin's list of virtues was similar to Aristotle in that good character was found at the midpoint between extremes of action or inaction.

Perhaps for the readers who failed to be "taught as if you taught them not," Franklin adopted the direct approach of a worldly elder statesman and presented a list of thirteen essential virtues with a brief clarifying description. He enumerated the virtues in order of importance; and the astute reader is reminded of the stories from part one where a lack of one of the qualities had been implicated in an erratum:

1. *Temperance.*

    Eat not to Dullness. Drink not to Elevation

2. *Silence.*

    Speak not but what may benefit others or yourself. Avoid trifling conversation.

3. *Order.*

    Let all things have their places. Let each part of your business have its time.

4. *Resolution.*

    Resolve to perform what you ought. Perform without fail what you resolve.

5. *Frugality.*

    Make no expense but to do good to others or yourself (i.e., waste nothing).

6. *Industry.*

> Lose no time. Be always employed in something useful. Cut off all unnecessary actions.

7. *Sincerity.*

> Use no hurtful deceit. Think innocently and justly; and if you speak; speak accordingly

8. *Justice.*

> Wrong none, by doing injuries or omitting the benefits that are your duty.

9. *Moderation.*

> Avoid extremes. Forbear resenting injuries so much as you think they deserve.

10. *Cleanliness.*

> Tolerate no uncleanliness in body, clothes, or habitation.

11. *Tranquility.*

> Be not disturbed at trifles, or at accidents common or unavoidable.

12. *Chastity.*

> Rarely use venery but for health or offspring; never to dullness, weakness, or the injury of your own or another's peace or reputation.

13. *Humility.*

> Imitate Jesus and Socrates.[50]

Franklin's humorous discussion of the rigorous program of record keeping he maintained for about a year with the hope of attaining moral perfection softens the presentation of prohibitions and moral imperatives. He would keep a chart of the virtues and at the end of each day give himself a black mark if he failed at living up to one of the virtues. There would also be a virtue of the week upon which he would focus particular effort. Perfection in morals may have been an impossible—even a ridiculous—goal admitted Franklin, "yet I was by the Endeavor made a better and a happier Man than I otherwise should have been, if I had not attempted it."[51]

He accepted Americans—as he accepted himself—as they were: materialistic, religiously self-directed, egocentric, determined, and practical. There was no condemnation or expectation that the earthier impulses would be eliminated; just suggestions that people endeavor to adopt habits of virtue and moderation. The emphasis was on the practicality of these behaviors as a means to the end of a happy life. At one time he had thought about expanding his list of virtues into a book called the *Art of Virtue* that would have shown the "Means & Manner of obtaining Virtue."[52] He claimed that he was too busy to complete the project. Perhaps it would have been too assertive, and the autobiography accomplished the same thing.[53] Then again, such a dogmatic book would have attracted critics and ultimately diminished his reputation. He observed that the published sermons of the eminent Great Awakening preacher George Whitefield provided grist to his enemies and his standing might have been improved if he had written less.[54]

Franklin's most ambitious project was to form an international party of virtue. Taking a figurative page from Plato's *Republic,* Franklin envisioned the possibility of a nation ruled by the most virtuous. He observed that few leaders "act with a View to the Good of Mankind"[55] and believed that a core group of wise individuals might, with proper instruction, work together to "work great changes . . . among Mankind."[56] The first recruits would declare their belief in an all-powerful God who rewarded virtue, and would practice the thirteen virtues. The endgame of this effort was the protection of freedom. For Franklin, there was a practical and inextricable connection between virtue and freedom. The virtuous person was "free from the Dominion of Vice;" an industrious and frugal person was "free from Debt, which exposes a Man to Confinement and a Species of Slavery to his Creditors."[57] Although he believed the project was feasible, he had been distracted by necessary business when he was younger, and when older he lacked the strength and energy to carry out a project of such magnitude.[58] Perhaps he believed that his compensation for having failed to accomplish this great project was his life long effort at instructing the common man. Franklin considered *Poor Richard's Almanack* to be the "proper Vehicle for conveying Instruction among the common People" that was filled with proverbs that would inculcate virtue.[59]

THE HEAD AND THE HEART

In *Notes on the State of Virginia,* Jefferson wrote of his anxieties concerning institution of slavery. He prophetically wrote, "I tremble for my country when I reflect that God is just: that his justice cannot sleep for ever" and he looked to the future "for a total emancipation, and that this is disposed, in the order of events, to be with the consent of the masters, rather than by their extirpation."[60] His problem with slavery, however, was not that it was injurious to the humanity of the slaves. He held that the main problem with slavery was the negative impact on the slaveholding class. The slaveholder was the ultimate victim of this labor system because it undermined good morals and moderation. "The whole commerce between master and slave is a perpetual exercise of the most boisterous passions," wrote Jefferson, "the most unremitting despotism on the one part, and degrading submissions on the other."[61]

The slaveholder provided a poor role model to his children when it came to the importance of regulating the passions. Reflecting either his personal experience or his observations, Jefferson wrote that "the parent storms, the child looks on, catches the lineaments of wrath, puts on the same airs in the circle of smaller slaves, gives loose to his worst passions, and thus nursed, educated, and daily exercised in tyranny, cannot but be a prodigy who can retain his manners and morals undepraved by such circumstances."[62] Jefferson believed that the presence of slaves undermined efforts at self-regulation that was so important to the virtuous life. His description was a graphic portrayal of the circumstances of power that are destructive to virtuous behavior and create tyrants.

The use of the word tyranny in the above passage should not be bypassed. On an individual scale, a tyrant was a person who was without morals. At the political level it was the leader who must not be allowed to rule. The climactic statement in the Declaration asserted that the bad character of the King of Great Britain made him "a Tyrant . . . unfit to be the ruler of a free people." Character mattered. On both the personal and political level, the willingness to apply the energy to prevent the proliferation of tyrants was not assured. Jefferson addressed this potential for lethargy in the Declaration when he wrote that "experience hath shewn, that mankind are more disposed to suffer, while evils are sufferable, than to right themselves by abolishing the forms to which they are accustomed." Just as it was a people's "right, it is their duty, to throw off such Government," it was also incumbent upon the citizens to resist the tyrant within. That was no easy task. Jefferson played an important role in disposing of the British tyrant, the story of his success at modulating the potential tyrant within was a bit murkier.

This is why one letter written in 1786 has attracted so much attention. The "Head and Heart letter" may be the only one in existence where Jefferson addressed his personal struggle with the polarities of passion and rationality. Did Jefferson think he was writing a letter that was meant for an audience beyond his love interest? Did the contents of the letter mean more to him than just an expression of personal longing? One might safely conclude that he did. Jefferson made a copy of this letter, which he did with most of his letters to help him remember what he had written and to whom. He was aware of how his written words would be important to posterity. The only letters we know that Jefferson destroyed, and were therefore meant to be kept completely private, were the letters between him and his wife.[63]

The letter was written after Maria Cosway, a married woman to whom he was deeply attracted, had departed from Paris. Suffering from a broken wrist that forced him to write with his off hand, the lovelorn

Jefferson produced a twelve-page letter constructed as a dialogue between his head and his heart. The head was utilitarian and selfishly calculating, while the passionately irrational and impulsive heart longed for social connections. Historians argue over whether the head or the heart came out the winner.[64] The letter ends with the heart having the last word, and for that reason some give the win to the heart. This was a love letter, after all, and Jefferson hoped to see the recipient again so perhaps too much is made of that.

The focus on who won, however, misses the point. It was an ongoing struggle. At any one point in time one part might dominate the other but there was never meant to be an ultimate winner. There would be no tyranny of either the head or the heart. A moderate balance between the two was the ideal. An overview of the letter makes it clear that to be dominated by either polarity would lead to misery. The head would discipline the irrational passions of the heart, and the work of the heart was to maintain social cohesion through promoting prosocial behavior. A balance must be found at the Aristotelian median point.

Jefferson wrote of the psyche as "a divided empire" with an amoral rational sense ameliorated by the demands of the heart where the moral sense resided. The heart speaking to the head maintained that, "when the circle is to be squared, or the orbit of a comet to be traced; when the arch of greatest strength, or the solid of least resistance is to be investigated, take you the problem," for the heart knows nothing of these problems. "In like manner in denying to you the feelings of sympathy, of benevolence, of gratitude, of justice, of love, of friendship, she has excluded you from their controul," continued the heart, "to these she has adapted the mechanism of the heart. Morals were too essential to the happiness of man to be risked on the uncertain combinations of the head."[65]

The head argued in turn for the importance of mental serenity and the need to calculate the rational benefit that might result from any behavior. Speaking to the mental anguish over the loss of his beguiling friend, the head reminded the heart of his earlier reluctance to risk a new relationship. "I never ceased whispering to you," scolded the head, "that we had no occasion for new acquaintance; that the greater their merit and talents, the more dangerous their friendship to our tranquility, because the regret at parting would be greater." The head drew from the teachings of Epicurus, and reminded the heart that "the art of life is the art of avoiding pain: and he is the best pilot who steers clearest of the rocks and shoals with which it is beset. Pleasure is always before us; but misfortune is at our side." The reclusive Jefferson has the head continue to remind the heart that "the most effectual means of being secure against pain is to retire within ourselves, and to suffice for our own happiness." A wise man will depend only on himself, "for nothing is ours which another may deprive us of." Only intellectual pleasures have value, for they will always be "leading us to something new . . . we ride, serene and sublime, above the concerns of this mortal world, contemplating truth and nature, matter and motion, the laws which bind up their existence, and that eternal being who made and bound them up by these laws. Let this be our employ." [66]

This assertion made by the head was balanced by the heart's moral sense that we must live connected with others. As the heart responded, "this world abounds indeed with misery: to lighten it's burthen we must divide it with one another. But let us now try the virtues of your mathematical balance, and as you have put into one scale the burthens of friendship, let me put its comforts into the other." The heart praised the comfort and encouragement that friendship provides, and with a hint of utilitarianism that the head would agree with, adds that "assuredly nobody will care for him who cares for nobody." [67] The heart reminds the head, that despite the current state of misery, most friendships involved more pleasure than pain. Connections with others, was ultimately a condition that would satisfy both the head and heart.

To emphasize the point that neither the head nor the heart was to overpower the other, the heart reminded the head of past errors in judgment. Jefferson made these mistakes when he ignored the importance of helping others. One occurred when he encountered a soldier on a road in the outskirts of Paris. The weary soldier asked for a ride in Jefferson's carriage but he turned him down after Jefferson calculated that there were too many soldiers on the road "and that if all should be taken up our horses would fail in their journey." He later regretted this decision and admitted to the faulty reasoning. It was not rational to conclude that if "we cannot relieve all the distressed we should relieve as many as we can." Another instance occurred in Philadelphia when a disheveled looking woman asked Jefferson for money. He dismissed her as drunkard. In a maxim that could just as easily be attributed to Franklin, Jefferson's heart chides him with the reminder that "those who want the dispositions to give, easily find reasons why they ought not to give." The heart later led Jefferson back to the woman and he gave her money that she immediately used to place her child in school. [68] Once again, the head had simply come to a faulty conclusion. To contribute to the education of children was a project of the utmost importance to Jefferson's understanding of how a well-ordered society could be maintained. In both of these cases the heart did not reject the process of rational calculation, only that the head had come to the wrong conclusions and the kindly inclinations of the heart helped to correct the mistake.

In the Declaration, Jefferson based the reasons for revolt in the rationality of the "Laws of Nature and of Nature's God." In this letter, however, Jefferson's heart takes some of the credit:

> If our country, when pressed with wrongs at the point of the bayonet, had been governed by its heads instead of its hearts, where should we

have been now? hanging on a gallows as high as Haman's. You began to calculate and to compare wealth and numbers: we threw up a few pulsations of our warmest blood: we supplied enthusiasm against wealth and numbers: we put our existence to the hazard, when the hazard seemed against us, and we saved our country: justifying at the same time the ways of Providence, whose precept is to do always what is right, and leave the issue to him. In short, my friend, as far as my recollection serves me, I do not know that I ever did a good thing on your suggestion, or a dirty one without it.[69]

Great deeds are accomplished when consequences are calculated by the head and the passions of the heart are engaged. This is the point of moderation where the virtuous path of righteous behavior is held in a delicate balance. In a letter written towards the end of his life, Jefferson wrote of the disaster that resulted for the French when their passions were not modulated, but indicated in addition that there were broader lessons to be learned:

> If ever, we are to guard against ourselves. not against ourselves as we are, but as we may be, for who can now imagine what we may become under circumstances not now imaginable? . . . Jacobins, in another country, was instituted on principles and views as virtuous as ever kindled the hearts of patriots. It was the pure patriotism of their purposes which extended their association to the limits of the nation, and rendered their, power within it boundless; and it was this power which degenerated their principles and practices to such enormities as never before could have been imagined.[70]

In this chapter a closer look was taken at the importance of virtue to the maintenance of liberty. This was a time when leaders knew that if one was not moral enough to govern themselves, then they could not be trusted with the governing of others. Two of the greatest thinkers of the revolutionary generation struggled to manage the tyrants within. Power in society must be balanced; the powers within the person must also be held in a delicate state of equilibrium. Franklin worked out his ideas and presented them to posterity by writing his autobiography. He discussed his errata as events that resulted from an imbalance between what was good and what had been momentarily convenient. His virtues were Aristotelian in that they aimed for a middle point between undesirable extremes. Jefferson has always been more impervious. There was one evening in October of 1786, however, when a heart (and wrist) broken Jefferson wrote a letter where he expressed his deepest feelings about human nature and the potentialities for trouble when the passions are not held in check. Perhaps when forced to write with his left-hand, Jefferson unconsciously gave us greater access to his more emotional right brain than under ordinary circumstances. The survival of liberty was psychologically challenging. It required that citizens be continually on guard against avaricious leaders as well as the corrupting impulses from within. The tyrant without was as dangerous as the tyrant within.

In this project I am suggesting that the founders understood liberty as consisting of four values that were linked together and defined the good life. Freedom meant the right to choose what one wanted to do and who the political leaders would be. One must have knowledge and understanding, however, to choose what is ultimately beneficial to the good life, otherwise freedom would not last. Internality impacted externality. These are abstract ideas that are only meaningful if it can be demonstrated that they affected behavior. Granted that the self-promoting writings of two of the more ambiguous of the founders does not reveal much beyond how they wanted to be perceived. Unless they are to be dismissed, however, as being the most manipulative of hypocrites, what they wrote should be accepted as expressing something about how they wished to live. Character mattered a great deal.

Franklin and Jefferson each expressed an understanding that freedom happened within a common space of reciprocity. It was a fragile state. Can the people structure a system of government that will both protect and nourish liberty? Are the people ethically strong enough not to abuse their personal and political liberty and undermine the public good? For a generation that set about the business of constructing new governments, these were not abstract questions. They lived their theories. In the next two chapters the urgent problems that the founders faced over how constitutions might actually answer those questions will be addressed.

NOTES

1. Charles Louis de Secondat de Montesquieu, *The Spirit of the Laws*, ed. Anne M. Cohler, Basia C. Miller, and Harold S. Stone (Cambridge: Cambridge University Press, 2009), 602.

2. Lester J. Cappon, ed., *The Adams-Jefferson Letters: The Complete Correspondence between Thomas Jefferson and Abigail and John Adams*, 1959 ed. (Chapel Hill: Univ. of North Carolina Press, 2001), 388.

3. Ibid.

4. Alexis de Tocqueville, "Part II: Chapter 5," *Democracy in America*, ed. Eduardo Nolla, trans. James T. Schleifer, English ed. (Indianapolis: Liberty Fund, 2012), 1:359.

5. Gordon S. Wood, *Revolutionary Characters: What Made the Founders Different* (New York: Penguin Books, 2007), 102.

6. Monticello, "Maria Cosway (Engraving)," Research and Collections, accessed February 4, 2018, https://www.monticello.org/site/research-and-collections/maria-cosway-engraving.

7. Dumas Malone, *Jefferson the Virginian*, vol. 1, *Jefferson and His Time* (Boston: Little, Brown and Company, 1948), 5.

8. Bernard Bailyn, *To Begin the World Anew: The Genius and Ambiguities of the American Founders* (New York: Alfred A. Knopf, 2003), 65.

9. Gordon S. Wood, *The Americanization of Benjamin Franklin* (New York: Penguin Press, 2005), 9.

10. Such as in 1782 after criticism of his behavior as governor of Virginia during the war, conflicts with Alexander Hamilton during Washington's administration, dis-

agreements with Adams when he served as vice president, and with most everything during the last months of his presidency.

11. Betty Goss, "Public Speakinig," Thomas Jefferson Encyclopedia, last modified January 9, 2001, accessed January 30, 2020, https://www.monticello.org/site/research-and-collections/public-speaking.

12. Gordon S. Wood, *The Creation of the American Republic: 1776–1787* (Chapel Hill: University of North Carolina Press, 1998), 52.

13. Wood, *Revolutionary Characters*, 71.

14. Jerry Weinberger, *Benjamin Franklin Unmasked: On the Unity of His Moral, Religious, and Political Thought* (Lawrence: University Press of Kansas, 2005), xii.

15. Christopher S. McClure, "Learning from Franklin's Mistakes: Self-Interest Rightly Understood in the Autobiography," *The Review of Politics* 76 (2014), 92.

16. Ibid., 72

17. Malone, *Jefferson, the Virginian*, 81.

18. Richard B. Bernstein, *Thomas Jefferson* (Oxford: Oxford University Press, 2005), 63.

19. Max Byrd, "The Brief History of a Historical Novel," *The Wilson Quarterly* 31, no. 4 (Autumn 2007): 26.

20. Bailyn, *To Begin the World Anew*, 37.

21. Ibid.

22. Jean M. Yarbrough, *American Virtues: Thomas Jefferson on the Character of a Free People* (Lawrence: University Press of Kansas, 1998), xix.

23. Steven Forde, "Benjamin Franklin's Autobiography and the Education of America," *The American Political Science Review* 86, no. 2 (June 1992): 357.

24. Richard D. Miles, "The American Image of Benjamin Franklin," *American Quarterly* 9, no. 2 (Summer 1957): 117.

25. Ibid, 118.

26. Weinberger, *Benjamin Franklin Unmasked*, xiv.

27. See Weinberger (2005).

28. John Adams' descendants, particularly Charles Francis Adams, carried on the campaign to diminish Franklin as morally corrupt and superficial. See Miles (1957).

29. John Adams, "From John Adams to Benjamin Rush, 4 April 1790," *Founders Online*, last modified June 29, 2017, accessed March 7, 2018, http://founders.archives.gov/documents/Adams/99-02-02-0903.

30. Richard D. Miles, "The American Image of Benjamin Franklin," *American Quarterly* 9, no. 2 (Summer 1957): 123–4.

31. Jennifer Jordan Baker, "Benjamin Franklin's Autobiography and the Credibility of Personality," *Early American Literature* 35, no. 3 (2000): 274–5.

32. Mulford, Carla. "Figuring Benjamin Franklin in American Cultural Memory." *The New England Quarterly* 72, no. 3 (1999): 423.

33. Benjamin Franklin, *Autobiography, Poor Richard, and Later Writings: Letters from London, 1757–1775, Paris, 1776–1785, Philadelphia, 1785–1790, Poor Richard's Almanack, 1733–1758, the Autobiography*, ed. Joseph A. Leo Lemay, 5th ed. (New York: Library of America, 2008), 567.

34. Ibid., 575.

35. Ibid.

36. Ibid., 580–81.

37. Ibid., 632.

38. McClure, "Learning from Franklin's Mistakes," 72.

39. Tocqueville, "Part II: Chapter 5," *Democracy in America*, 1:365.

40. Franklin, *Autobiography*, 607.

41. Ibid.

42. Ibid., 606.

43. Ibid., 619.

44. Ibid.

45. Ibid.

46. Ibid.
47. Ibid., 582.
48. Ibid., 634.
49. Ibid., 635–36.
50. Ibid., 644–45.
51. Ibid., 650–1.
52. Ibid., 652.
53. McClure, "Learning from Franklin's Mistakes," 87.
54. Franklin, *Autobiography*, 670.
55. Ibid., 655.
56. Ibid., 657.
57. Ibid., 656.
58. Or perhaps, as Plato had worried, he was never willing to set aside his own personal happiness long enough to work towards the greater goal of the happiness and well-being of the community.
59. Franklin, *Autobiography*, 657.
60. Thomas Jefferson, "Notes on the State of Virginia," 1787, in *The Portable Thomas Jefferson*, ed. Merrill D. Peterson (New York: Penguin Books, 1977), 215.
61. Ibid., 214.
62. Ibid., 215.
63. James Hershman, "Jefferson's Head and Heart letter," e-mail message to author, February 4, 2018.
64. Jeremy Engels, "Disciplining Jefferson: The Man within the Breast and the Rhetorical Norms of Producing Order," *Rhetoric & Public Affairs* 9, no. 3 (Fall 2006): 413.
65. Thomas Jefferson, "From Thomas Jefferson to Maria Cosway, 12 October 1786," *Founders Online*, National Archives, last modified June 29, 2017, accessed November 8, 2017, https://founders.archives.gov/documents/Jefferson/01-10-02-0309.
66. Ibid.
67. Ibid.
68. Ibid.
69. Ibid.
70. Thomas Jefferson, "From Thomas Jefferson to Jedidiah Morse, 6 March 1822," *Founders Online*, National Archives, last modified June 29, 2017, accessed November 16, 2017, http://founders.archives.gov/documents/Jefferson/98-01-02-2700.

SEVEN

Virtue or Rights?

To be free implies a lifestyle. For the founders it meant a constancy of effort to be virtuous. Virtue not only mattered; it was the central pillar upon which the survival of a nation of free citizens depended. The founders' central truth was that a commitment to moral principles was the essence of good character and without good character, all was lost. Realistically, however, the founders knew that the hard work of character building would not be carried out by everyone equally. Nature, after all, had not been equitable in her distribution of good sense. Aside from the logistical impracticalities, this was the main reason the founders preferred a representative republic over a democracy. Men of high character would be recognized by their fellow citizens and be selected to lead. These men of virtue, understanding the importance of service to the community, would answer the call. The good would rise to the top.

The next two chapters will address the critical period between 1787 and 1789 when the American people recognized the need for an adjustment to the system of government that had been established by the Articles of Confederation. That system had left too much power in the hands of those who had proven themselves to be ill-equipped. The second attempt at government—the United States Constitution—corrected the structural flaws of the Articles by placing more power in the national government, therefore, and hopefully, in the hands of the more virtuous elite.

Yet a far more subtle and profoundly important shift also occurred at that time. During the ratification debate between the Constitution's advocates and critics—the so-called federalists and antifederalists—the debate focused on both virtue and rights. Virtue lost some ground; rights moved to the center. This began the slow transformation that has led to the present day understanding of liberty. It is all about rights without moral responsibilities, and it is up to the moral guidance of the elected representatives to solve the biggest problems.

The antifederalists were concerned that the Constitution shifted too much power to the national government. The prefix of anti to their label was unfortunate and misleading. They were not against federalism. They believed in a federalist system where power would be divided between a national government and state governments. They were against particular aspects of the Constitution that appeared to threaten personal and political liberty. Not only would the will of the people be greatly limited in the newly structured national government, but this new center of power could crush the liberties of the people. These fears ultimately led to the addition to the Constitution of ten specific guarantees of individual liberty known as the Bill of Rights. Unfortunately, this emphasis on rights without the expectation of virtue represented a significant shift away from the original idea of liberty.

As the idealistic revolutionaries aged off of center stage, the political dialogue was dominated by the more practical minded of the next generation. The apprehensions of the latter allowed them to succeed in establishing a consolidated government with enhanced power. Perhaps Americans were not the most virtuous people after all, and therefore not capable of sustaining the freedom that they had so recently won. With the ratification of the Constitution, the expectation diminished that liberty would only flourish if the citizens were virtuous. Tremendous faith was placed in the belief that the elected leaders would be men of good character.

Political liberty was reined in as the influence that the citizens had upon two and half of the three branches of the national government (the executive, judicial, and upper house of Congress) would be minimal. Political liberty was devalued for safety to be ensured. Along with this shift in power, something important was happening to happiness. The back-and-forth between the federalists and antifederalists was not just a wrestling over the why and how of structuring a balanced government. The heartfelt conversation between the federalists and antifederalists was a continuation of the search for truth concerning the human potential that reaches back to antiquity.

This was their shared truth: God meant for people to live free and to treat one another as equals, to be secure in their property, and to pursue happiness. The Creator had endowed humankind with a rational mind. If that mind was properly focused, folks would realize that virtuous living would promote the good life. Civil society was established so that God's will for people could be carried out. We willingly gave-up some of our freedoms to ensure that all citizens could live with comfort and security. John Locke wrote, and the founders declared, that to protect these natural rights was the essential feature of good government. To create a government that protected freedom, promoted human flourishing, and assured security was to be carrying out God's work. Perhaps that was why John Adams referred to politics "as the divine science" in that it was "the science of social happiness, and the blessings of society depend entirely on the constitutions of government."[1] Establishing this "social happiness" by finding an agreed upon balance between promoting liberty and protecting security has been an elusive goal. In Locke's state of nature, it had been the abuse of liberty on the part of a few transgressors and the threat to the safety of all that required the loss of some freedoms. The problem of balancing these two values—liberty and security—has determined much of the history of the United States.

At certain crisis points in our nation's history the conflict has become so powerful that it resulted in an alteration to our constitutional form of government. These were times when the ideological girders that support government were shaken and some feared the entire structure could come crashing down. The response has always been to increase the powers of the federal government. The first example of this was when the nation's original attempt at government failed. Historians refer to the time when the sovereign states were knit together by the Articles of Confederation as the critical period. There arose a belief that the young republic was failing. The lynchpin of liberty—virtue-based happiness among the people at large—did not seem to be adequately widespread, and so the country adopted a new constitution. The fact that the weightiest of words—happiness—was not written anywhere in the United States Constitution was emblematic of this change.

The revised plan replaced the Articles of Confederation. The new constitution, as stated in the preamble, would produce "a more perfect Union, establish Justice, insure domestic Tranquility, provide for the common defense, promote the general Welfare, and secure the Blessings of Liberty to ourselves and our Posterity." What about happiness? A word that was so pervasive during the revolutionary period had vanished in the US Constitution of 1787. The founders' emphasis—if not obsession—with happiness had been illustrative of what the expanded liberty that they worked for would both necessitate and nurture: a virtuous citizenry. The omission of this one word so heavily weighted with history and meaning—that was omnipresent in the letters, speeches, and pamphlets of the revolutionary period—was significant. It was indicative of the transformation from the heady days of the Revolution, when the founders dreamed of a utopia of liberty, to the reality of a citizenry that perhaps was not so virtuous after all.

Chapter 2 investigated the meaning of happiness as a key concept in the Declaration; and it must be reemphasized that it was central to so many revolutionary publications. In the following example the very sober John Adams comes across as veritably giddy with hope that the republican government that could be established in America would be the pinnacle for mankind. In his highly influential pamphlet *Thoughts on*

Government Adams wrote (italics added) that "the *happiness* of society is the end of government, as all Divines and moral Philosophers will agree that the *happiness* of the individual is the end of man." He continued,

> From this principle it will follow, that the form of government, which communicates ease, comfort, security, or in one word *happiness* to the greatest number of persons, and in the greatest degree, is the best. . . . All sober enquiries after truth, ancient and modern, Pagan and Christian, have declared that the *happiness* of man, as well as his dignity consists in virtue. Confucius, Zoroaster, Socrates, Mahomet, not to mention authorities really sacred, have agreed in this . . . a form of government then, whose principle and foundation is virtue, will not every sober man acknowledge it better calculated to promote the general *happiness* than any other form? . . . When! Before the present epocha, had three millions of people full power and a fair opportunity to form and establish the wisest and *happiest* government that human wisdom can contrive?[2]

It would be expected, therefore, that in 1787 the word happiness might continue to be prominent in the US Constitution. Certainly, the fitting place to remind of the importance of happiness would be in the preamble to the Constitution. It was not there. Instead of Jefferson's *pursuit* the Constitution will *promote*, but now *happiness* has morphed into *general welfare*. Perhaps the better place to look might be Article I, Section 8, where the specific duties of the national government were enumerated. The first paragraph begins with a statement about how taxes will be justified: "to pay the Debts and provide for the common defense and general welfare of the United States." It appears that "general welfare" has indeed replaced happiness as the broadest goal of government. Where was happiness?

The mystery of why happiness was not mentioned in the Constitution has not been widely investigated. It is not a trivial oversight. They did not simply forget.[3] Nor does the evidence support the idea that statements about happiness simply do not belong in constitutions. The opening efforts at constitution writing were undertaken at the state level. In May of 1776 the Continental Congress instructed the states to compose new constitutions eradicating all relationships with Great Britain. New Hampshire had a jump on the movement and in January of 1776 was already organizing a new government while still expressing hope that the conflict with Great Britain could be resolved. The Continental Congress had not yet voted for independence which might be why New Hampshire only mentioned happiness in the negative, in reference to the current circumstances with Great Britain: "[We] have taken into our serious consideration the unhappy circumstances . . . we conceive ourselves reduced to the necessity of establishing A FORM OF GOVERNMENT to continue during the present unhappy and unnatural contest with Great Britain."[4]

It is widely believed that Jefferson's words in the Declaration of Independence were at least in part influenced by George Mason's language in the Virginia Constitution concerning man's inherent rights. Mason had written, that citizens had rights to "the enjoyment of life and liberty, with the means of acquiring and possessing property, and pursuing and obtaining happiness and safety."[5] After publication of the Declaration, the state constitution writers chose to paraphrase Jefferson's invocation of happiness. The constitutions of New York, New Jersey, and Georgia all set out to create governments that would "best conduce to the happiness and safety of their constituents."[6] The North Carolinians anticipated that their government would be "most conducive to their happiness and prosperity."[7] The first lines of Pennsylvania's new Constitution supply the best evidence that Jefferson's words (if not his talent for graceful writing) were echoing in the Pennsylvanians' thoughts:

> WHEREAS all government ought to be instituted . . . to enable the individuals who compose it to enjoy their natural rights . . . and whenever these great ends of government are not obtained, the people have a right, by common consent to change it, and take such measures as to them may appear necessary to promote their safety and happiness.[8]

The fact of the existence of thirteen written constitutions with the majority of them specifically mentioning happiness is particularly remarkable when it is recalled that by 1778 the only written constitutions in the world existed in these thirteen states.[9]

Helpful in this discussion is a book by Professor of Literature Vivasvan Soni, *Mourning Happiness*. Soni wrote of the eighteenth century's "dramatic and unprecedented" obsession with happiness that was "a perennial favorite among essayists and pamphleteers in the period, resulting in a deluge of writing about happiness." "Many of the period's boldest and most innovative thinkers," continued Soni, "thrilled to the allure of a new age in which human happiness would matter before all else. The quest for a politics of happiness is evident in the distinctive concern for 'public happiness,' which engaged Rousseau, Jefferson, and Chastellux among others."[10]

Soni also remarked on the perplexing absence of happiness from the Constitution. Why were a people who had been so obsessed with the concept of happiness become so suddenly reticent?[11] According to Soni, by the late eighteenth century the classical Greek idea of happiness (*eudaimonia*) as a style of virtuous living, well-being, or flourishing that could be judged objectively was changing. Happiness had become a private, affective state that could only be judged individually; an idea we are more familiar with today. This can be seen, for example, in the rise of sentimentalism, a late eighteenth- and early nineteenth-century philosophical and literature movement.

This chapter provides an alternative, though not contradictory, explanation for the absence of happiness in the Constitution. The omission of "happiness" was not simply rhetorical, for "general welfare" was not conceptually interchangeable with "happiness." The loss of this important word symbolized the dawning realization that the functioning of government could not rely on virtuous citizens.

In previous chapters the theory has been advanced that for the founders, the liberty construct captured four important experiences, and happiness and liberty were inextricably connected. The idealized free citizen was virtuous and self-regulating, and experienced his God-given personal and political freedom in a socially productive manner. The founders therefore used the word happiness in an Aristotelian sense: happiness was a style of virtuous living that could be habituated through reason and practice. Virtuous citizens possessed the self-regulation to exist comfortably and securely under the auspices of the relatively light-hand of government. Honorable and moral citizens would promote good government; good government would encourage and inspire virtue in the people.

John Adams pointed out this reciprocity between the virtuous citizen and good government when he sketched out the ideal design of a government that was founded on the proper principles:

> [Good government] introduces knowledge among the People, and inspires them with a conscious dignity, becoming Freemen. A general emulation takes place, which causes good humor, sociability, good manners, and good morals to be general. That elevation of sentiment, inspired by such a government, makes the common people brave and enterprising. That ambition which is inspired by it makes them sober, industrious and frugal. You will find among them some elegance, perhaps, but more solidity; a little pleasure, but a great deal of business—some politeness, but more civility. If you compare such a country with the regions of domination, whether Monarchial or Aristocratical, you will fancy yourself in Arcadia or Elisium.[12]

Following Adams' conclusions, if Arcadian harmony was not widespread it may have been due to the fact that the government the Americans had constructed after the Revolution was not structured correctly. A new constitution would bring about a needed correction. In the intervening decade between Adams' pamphlet and the Constitution, however, a change took place in the optimism that a minimal government authority could ensure happiness and safety for the people.

The Confederation Congress adopted the Articles of Confederation in 1777. The Congress was the central governing authority that was designed to hold together the sovereign states in a firm league of friendship. Within just a few years, according to many observers such as James Madison, the Confederation appeared to be, "so thin as to be incompetent to the dispatch of the more important business before them."[13] The belief that had inspired the Revolution was that the republic based on expanded liberty would only survive if the citizens were virtuous, but it looked to some that the state legislatures had been seized by unvirtuous political mediocrities. The middling class was being elected into the newly reconstituted state legislatures, appalling many members of the old ruling elite. The Articles of Confederation left the centralized authority with no power to stabilize events within the states.

The most pressing problem, the same problem that has confronted all new republics after throwing off their imperialistic oppressors, was an economic crisis. The Confederation Congress could not directly tax the citizens; it could only request revenue from the states. As it turned out, the revolutionaries who initially rallied around the cause of a tax revolt, did not necessarily become great tax collectors themselves. The state governments with their fumbling efforts at dealing with currency issues were adding to the problem. Debtors and poor farmers, who generally lived in the more western regions of the states, were having trouble paying their taxes and were in danger of losing their farms.

Economic misery precipitated violent revolts in many of the states. During the summer of 1787 the Virginia state legislature passed a new tax with the intent of paying off the war debt. In Greenbriar County rebels burned the county court house and vowed not to pay. The most famous revolt by poor western farmers was led by Daniel Shays in Massachusetts, a state that had experienced years of factional conflicts and was suffering a particularly severe economic depression. Shays was a veteran of Lexington, Bunker Hill, and Saratoga; and for all his patriotic service had received no compensation. Burdened with debt and taxes that could not be paid, Shays led an angry mob to close down the court house to prevent foreclosures on their farms. Shays' Rebellion was the momentous proximal event to the call for a convention to revise the Articles of Confederation.

Was there a widespread failure of the state governments to carry out the most important duty of government: protect individual rights and promote happiness? Was the parade of horribles leading the fledgling republic to collapse, or was the country relatively stable and the catastrophizing overwrought?[14] Were the deplorables ruining the states? Determining the degrees of dreadful cannot possibly be resolved today if the folks living at the time could not agree. We seem no better in the present, after all, with immediate and constant communication, to distinguish facts from opinion or to avoid succumbing to confirmation bias in the search for truth. Consider for example the contrary perspectives from two Virginians from the years 1787 and 1788 respectively.

James Madison did not pull any punches when he discussed the state legislatures. They were "evil." They failed to respond to requisitions from Congress. They encroached upon the federal authority by ignoring foreign treaties and forming separate treaties with the Indians. As a result of "the sphere of life from which most of their members are taken, and the circumstances under which their legislative business is carried on," the state legislatures were trespassing "on the rights of each other" which was "destructive of the general harmony." The multiple and continually changing laws passed by the state legislatures "prove a want of wisdom" and "their injustice betrays a defect still more alarming . . . it brings more into question the fundamental principle of republican Government, that the majority who rule in such Governments, are the safest Guardians both of public Good and of private rights."[15]

The cause of the evil was that the state representatives were motivated by ambition and personal interest and not with protecting the welfare of the people. They were absolutely lacking in virtue. Subsequent elections failed to "displace the offenders, and repair the mischief" because the voters were deluded and convinced that the "base and selfish measures" were for the public good. "Varnishing his sophistical arguments with the glowing colors of popular eloquence" candidates deceived the unwary.[16] Not even the religious oaths of office were helping to restrain the immoral actions, for "the conduct of every popular assembly acting on oath . . . proves that individuals join without remorse in acts, against which their consciences would revolt if proposed to them under the like sanction, separately in their closets."[17]

Madison's fellow Virginian Patrick Henry did not agree that the times were so dire. According to Henry, the hoped for moral and social improvement that would follow the revolution had been gloriously achieved. Rights were protected, property was safe, and the charges against the states were groundless. "Public and private security are to be found here in the highest degree," wrote Henry. The free people of our country should "not be intimidated by imaginary dangers." "Fear is the passion of slaves," he continued, "our political and natural hemisphere are now equally tranquil."[18]

Although many of the antifederalists agreed that there were a few problems pertaining to currency and commerce that should be addressed, the current form of government "was the best calculated of any form hitherto, to secure the rights of our persons and of our property, and that the general circumstances of the people show an advanced state of improvement never before shown."[19] The antifederalists claimed that the federalists were representing the situation to be "so *critically* dreadful" in order to frighten the people into accepting a radically new plan of government, "however reprehensible and exceptionable the proposed plan of government may be." Citizens needed to be wary about the warnings of danger because those who "want a man to change his condition" will describe it as "miserable, wretched, and despised; and draw a pleasing picture of that which we would have him assume."[20] To be "criminally alarming our fears" was "the argument of tyrants."[21] Europe was not threatening security, and the domestic situation was not so dreadful as to hurry the people into a new form of government.[22]

The crucial point, however, was that many of the most respected leaders, such as George Washington and Benjamin Franklin, believed that times were indeed critical. The founders understood current events within historic context that highlighted the fact that all governments that had expanded political liberty were inherently fragile and had fallen into oppression and corruption. It was incumbent upon the more virtuous citizens to be watchful for signs of vice that inevitably infected the people and be ready to institute reform in order to protect liberty, happiness, and safety. History had taught that leaders can be latent enemies and all political communities were potential mobs. They did not just worry about the ever-present threats to liberty. They anticipated a crisis. Through their vigilance and willingness to address the problems of government they would be carrying forward with the work of the men who fought the Revolution. The fight with England had been a fight for liberty. Liberty was again threatened; but this time from within. The source was different but the problem was eternal: liberty was fragile.

In 1787 Jefferson wrote from Paris about the necessity for the people to always preserve a "spirit of resistance." "Lethargy" he wrote, was "the forerunner of death to public liberty." Although his statement that "the tree of liberty must be refreshed from time to time with the blood of patriots & tyrants"[23] may appear overwrought to the present-day reader, it was an accurate expression of the eighteenth-century belief that the survival of liberty required a fearless and unyielding exertion of effort on the part of its guardians. It would be a never-ending test to determine whether or not Americans were truly up to the task. If they failed, reflected Alexander Hamilton, it would not just be a misfortune for America, but for all of mankind.[24]

A belief in progress and the ability to analyze problems with fresh evidence and reason were the twin pillars of the Enlightenment. The first attempt at government was not protecting liberty, a new constitution would do a better job: progress. Hamilton wrote that the history of Greece and Italy fill one with "horror and disgust" and their stories have been used by despots to dismiss all attempts at free government as unable to maintain order.[25] The cause of liberty, however, would continue to expand because the original designs had been improved by modern minds. Hamilton captured this spirit of the Enlightenment when he assured his readers of the progress made in the science of politics. "The efficacy of various principles is now well understood," wrote Hamilton, "which were either not known at all, or imperfectly known to the ancients." Power can be checked and balanced by distributing it into separate departments; the courts are composed of judges who only hold office for good behavior, the people are represented in the legislature: "these are wholly new discoveries, or have made their principal progress towards perfection in modern times."[26]

It was not only the glory of America to be carrying forward the greatest cause for mankind, but also to be given the opportunity to continue with enlightened innovation. To cling to what we were comfortable with was contrary to the true spirit of the Revolution. This Enlightenment belief in progressive improvement encouraged them to seize opportunities for innovation. They could fearlessly reject, for example, the outdated certainty of a Montesquieu who had counseled against the establishment of a unified republic over a large territory. Hamilton wrote that although they have paid a decent respect to history, "they have not suffered a blind veneration for antiquity." The Americans were now destined to set an example to the world with innovations that have never been tried before.[27]

With their optimistic belief in the benefits of innovation, and their ability to improve their system of government, a group of concerned representatives from five states met in Annapolis, Maryland to discuss the current crisis in September of 1786. They determined that another meeting should be called in May of the following year:

> That there are important defects in the system of the Federal Government is acknowledged by the Acts of all those States. . . . That the defects, upon a closer examination, may be found greater and more numerous . . . your Commissioners are of opinion, that a Convention of Deputies from the different States, for the special and sole purpose of entering into this investigation, and digesting a plan for supplying such defects as may be discovered to exist.[28]

Although Madison admitted that "what may be the result of this political experiment cannot be foreseen,"[29] some of the most brilliant men to have ever lived at one time—James Madison, Benjamin Franklin, Alexander Hamilton, James Wilson, John Dickinson, George Wythe—collected in Philadelphia to address the "defects." A little over three months later a freshly drafted Constitution was submitted to the states for ratification.

After two hundred years, this document is viewed as the most stable protector of personal and political liberty ever written and a template for good government everywhere. It can therefore be difficult to understand how the Constitution could have been ratified by only the thinnest of margins and that many regarded it as a threat to their liberty. "I feel it among the first distresses that have happened to me in my life" wrote Richard Henry Lee to Washington "that I find myself compelled by irresistible conviction of mind to doubt about the new System for federal government . . . in consequence of long reflection upon the nature of Man and of government, that I am led to fear the danger that will ensue to Civil Liberty from the adoption of the new system."[30]

The opinions about the Constitution were diverse and ranged on a continuum of support and should not simply be boxed into categories of for or against. For purposes of simplification, two positions have been labeled by historians as either federalists or antifederalists. As stated above, whether the times were indeed so calamitous was a matter of opinion. Consistency would require that for those who saw no disease, no curative would be required. During the ratification debate the worldviews became more polarized as opinions on the Constitution were determined by a conflict over where they saw the greatest threats to liberty to be originating. Not only did the federalists believe that a lack of virtue was leading to recklessness in government, but that only the virtuous citizens, will admit that the legislative bodies under the Articles were unstable.[31] A lack of virtue in the citizenry was both a cause of the problems and was obscuring their ability to see that there was a problem.

The antifederalists, on the other hand, feared for their rights. In one important way the argument between the federalist and antifederalist begins with an agreement. If people were virtuous enough to conform to the laws of nature and to simply get along, no government would be needed. Madison wrote "if men were angels, no government would be necessary,"[32] and the antifederalist writing under the pseudonym Brutus agreed. Brutus wrote that if men "had been disposed to conform themselves to the rule of immutable righteousness, government would not have been requisite."[33] People cannot be trusted so government was necessary, but it logically followed that government created by people cannot be trusted either.

Liberty was the potential victim of tyranny, and tyranny could come from the top down or the bottom up. Increasing the power of government while reducing the people's political liberty can end with an authoritarian government and a loss of personal liberty; unbridled liberty among the people can lead to decadence, chaos and the rise of a demagogue. The solution hinged on virtue. If the founders continued to believe that the American people were the most virtuous citizens to have ever experienced freedom, then no increase in the power of government was necessary. The evidence did not support that position. If the citizens could be convinced that the leaders will be people of good character, and there are mechanisms to assure that will happen, then there is less worry over increasing the power of the national government. That was what the federalist needed to do.

NOTES

1. John Adams, "Thoughts on Government (April 1776)," The Adams Papers Digital Editions, accessed January 19, 2018, https://www.masshist.org/publications/apde2/view?&id=PJA04dg2.

2. Adams, "Thoughts on Government."

3. According to Alexander Hamilton's biographer Ron Chernow, "when [Hamilton] was asked why the framers omitted the word God from the Constitution, he replied, 'We forgot.'"—perhaps apocryphal. Ron Chernow, *Alexander Hamilton* (New York: Penguin Books, 2005), 235. The omission of any reference to God in the Constitution is interesting and tangentially related to the omission of happiness. The Declaration had made it clear that this was a statement of purpose by a people who were directed by God.

4. "New Hampshire Constitution (1776)," The Avalon Project: Documents in Law, History, and Diplomacy, accessed March 8, 2018, http://avalon.law.yale.edu/18th_century/nh09.asp.

5. "Virginia Declaration of Rights," The Avalon Project: Documents in Law, History, and Diplomacy, accessed March 7, 2018, http://avalon.law.yale.edu/18th_century/virginia.asp.

6. Ibid.

7. Ibid.

8. Ibid.

9. Donald S. Lutz, *The Origins of American Constitutionalism* (Baton Rouge: Louisiana State University Press, 1988), 1.

10. Vivasvan Soni, *Mourning Happiness: Narrative and the Politics of Modernity* (Ithaca: Cornell University Press, 2010), 3.

11. Soni, *Mourning Happiness*, 3.

12. Adams, "Thoughts on Government."

13. James Madison, "From James Madison to Thomas Jefferson, 19 March 1787," *Founders Online*, last modified November 26, 2017, accessed January 25, 2018, https://founders.archives.gov/documents/Madison/01-09-02-0169.

14. Michael Lienesch, "Historical Theory and Political Reform: Two Perspectives on Confederation Politics," *The Review of Politics* 45, no. 1 (January 1983): 94–95.

15. James Madison, "Vices of the Political System of the United States (1787)," National Humanities Center, accessed August 15, 2015, http://americainclass.org/sources/makingrevolution/constitution/text1/madisonvices.pdf.

16. Ibid.

17. Ibid.

18. Patrick Henry, "Speeches of Patrick Henry in the Virginia State Ratifying Convention, 7 June 1788," in *The Anti-Federalist: Writings by the Opponents of the Constitution*, ed. Herbert J. Storing and Murray Dry, (Chicago: University of Chicago Press, 1985), 306.

19. Agrippa, "To the People (3 December 1787)," in *The Anti-Federalist*, 235.

20. Federal Farmer, "Letter I (October 8, 1787)," in *The Anti-Federalist*, 34.

21. Agrippa, "To the People of Massachusetts (27 November 1787)," in *The Anti-Federalist*, 232.

22. "Centinel, Letter I (October 1787)," in *The Anti-Federalist*, 13.

23. Thomas Jefferson, "Thomas Jefferson to William Stephens Smith, November 13, 1787," Jefferson Quotes and Family Letters, accessed January 24, 2018, http://tjrs.monticello.org/letter/100.

24. Alexander Hamilton, "No. 1," in *The Federalist Papers : The Gideon Edition*, ed. James McClellan and George W. Carey, Gideon ed. (Indianapolis: Liberty Fund, 2001), 1.

25. Hamilton, "No. 9," in *The Federalist Papers*, 37.

26. Ibid., 38.

27. Hamilton, "No. 14," in *The Federalist Papers*, 67.

28. National Archives, "Annapolis Convention. Address of the Annapolis Convention, (14 September 1786)," *Founders Online*, accessed March 9, 2018, https://founders.archives.gov/documents/Hamilton/01-03-02-0556.

29. James Madison, "From James Madison to Thomas Jefferson, 19 March 1787," *Founders Online*, last modified November 26, 2017, accessed January 25, 2018, https://founders.archives.gov/documents/Madison/01-09-02-0169.

30. Richard Henry Lee, "To George Washington from Richard Henry Lee, 11 October 1787," *Founders Online*, last modified November 26, 2017, accessed January 25, 2018, http://founders.archives.gov/documents/Washington/04-05-02-0336.
31. Madison, "No. 10," in *The Federalist Papers*, 42.
32. Madison, "No. 51," in *The Federalist Papers*, 269.
33. Brutus, "To the Citizens of the State of New York, 1 November 1787," in *The Anti-Federalist*, 118.

EIGHT
More Need of Masters

In April of 1787, one month before the constitutional convention got underway, Benjamin Franklin wrote, "that only a virtuous people are capable of freedom. As nations become corrupt and vicious, they have more need of masters." Franklin believed that things were going about as well as could be expected "after so great an overturning." There have been some "disorders in different parts of the country," Franklin observed, "but we arrange them as they arise, and are daily mending and improving; so that I have no doubt but all will come right in time.[1] Franklin could not have known that the "mending and improving" would soon involve a reduction in the political liberty the citizens had experienced under the Articles of Confederation.

The constitutional revolution of 1787 was a restoration of virtue that many feared had been lost during the first attempt at governing the nation. The premise of the federalists' argument was that the power placed in the strengthened national government was less likely to be abused than it had been in the state governments. The burden of virtue was shifted away from the average citizen and to the leadership. There was no doubt that "aristocratical principles" were important to the new plan.[2] It was believed that men selected to govern under the proposed Constitution would be more virtuous, more trustworthy, and more rational, than the average. Whereas Locke had established the rationale and expectations for government, the federalists raised the stakes for what it meant to be a leader. Their writings represented a theory concerning lowered expectations of virtue in the citizenry and a return to the ancient Greek and Roman idealization of the leader.

THE ANTIFEDERALISTS

The principle grievance that activated the antifederalists was their certainty that the federalists were hijacking the spirit of the Revolution. The belief that the proposed Constitution was placing the nation on the road to despotism was the leitmotif of the antifederalists' writings. The Constitution has many "deformities" observed Patrick Henry, "it has an awful squinting; it squints towards monarchy."[3] They interpreted the actions of the federalists in the light of history. Henry warned that the move to strip the people of their liberties by the ambitions of a few had happened in Europe, ancient Greece, ancient and Rome.[4]

Ratification of the Constitution would amount to nothing short of catastrophe. From their standpoint, the proposed plan of government was designed to completely change the status of the people by placing excessive power in the national government.[5] All of privileges and blessings of liberty were at stake, warned the dissenters, as rights would "be sacrificed at the shrine of despotism" and "the shackles of slavery" would be riveted "on you and your unborn posterity."[6] The antifederalists believed that increasing the authority of the national government was a slippery slope of ever growing power. "Those who have governed," it was argued, "have been found in all ages ever active to enlarge their powers and abridge the public liberty."[7]

The antifederalists warned of the trickery of those who were moving with such haste to restructure the relationship between the states and the national government. They believed that it was the work of an unscrupulous yet well organized and highly energized minority. In that the antifederalists tended to downplay the current problems, they saw nefarious motives in those who advocated for a radical change.[8] They were arrogant and dishonest; they were tricking the people into depriving them of their liberties; they were the wealthy and ambitious who believe they have a right to dominate their fellow citizens; they were scheming for power. Those who had first called for the convention had been deceptive with their stated purpose. They had said they were only going to address a few of the problems pertaining to currency and commerce. The people had assumed that the convention would result in an assortment of amendments to the federal system. Had the people of the states known that the convention would bring about a total change, states would probably not have sent any delegates.[9] As no mention had originally been made of abandoning the old constitution and writing a new one, the states did not know "they were passing the Rubicon" when they sent members to the convention in Philadelphia.[10]

Though the antifederalists admitted that many honorable and virtuous republican men attended the convention, such as the irreproachable Washington, their number had not been sufficient. Once gathered, some of the delegates left Philadelphia when they realized that the convention was going well beyond the stated purpose. "Whilst the gilded chains were forging in the secret conclave," others continued to alarm "the fears of the people with dangers which did not exist, and exciting their hopes of greater advantages from the expected plan than even the best government on earth could produce."[11] The most scandalous accusation that the antifederalists could hurl at their opponents was that they were European in their sentiments. Perhaps because they had been educated in Europe, or were influenced by foreigners, "if we look upon the [federalists] we shall find some of their leaders to have formed pretty strong attachments to foreign nations," wrote one antifederalist.[12]

The antifederalists argued that it was incorrect to accept the theory that the checks and balances among the proposed three branches of the national government would protect the liberty of the people, or prevent an unlimited increase in the size and power of the national government in relation to the states. The equilibrium among the three branches would not last and power would eventually "preponderate to one or the other body," this would cause an eventual accumulation of all power in one branch. The antifederalists argued that both Congress and the Supreme Court would expand their powers overtime. Article I, Section 8, Clause 18 gave Congress power "to make all Laws which shall be necessary and proper for carrying into Execution the foregoing Powers, and all other Powers vested by this Constitution in the Government of the United States, or in any Department or Officer thereof" and would be used to expand the powers of taxation for any purpose that might "be for the *general welfare*." It was impossible to have a clear understanding of how far the powers could be stretched in the future, "or of the extent and number of the laws which may be deemed necessary and proper."[13]

The people might hope "that a wise and prudent congress will pay respect to the opinions of a free people . . . but a congress of a different character" might not respect those principles.[14] The antifederalists placed little faith in the virtuous self-restraint or good character of the future leaders as they pondered the meaning of "necessary and proper." Future administrations would probably look to expand their influence and "take every occasion to multiply laws, and officers to execute them, considering these as so many props for its own support." Taxes would be increased "to support the government, and to discharge foreign demands."[15] "The expense of the new plan [was] terrifying" with all the new complexities and inconveniences created by expanding the national level of government.[16]

The Supreme Court and the Senate would certainly expand their power. Armed with the knowledge of how the courts in England with "ingenious sophisms" had expanded their authority, it was predicted that the judicial branch would also extend "the sphere of influence."[17] The term of six years with no term limits for senators would make it probable, "from their extensive means of influence," that they would continue in office for life. The entire plan of government, therefore, was certainly going to result in "a permanent aristocracy."[18] Contributing to the foreseeable increase in the power of the national government was the complexity of the system. "If you complicate the plan by various orders, the people will be perplexed . . . about the source of abuses or misconduct" and the judgment of the people will be inoperable. The protection of liberty required that the sources of abuse be easily identifiable and that short terms in office will permit the people to quickly discard them at the next election.[19]

The antifederalists believed that the chief danger of the new plan was that liberty could only be protected through local government and that the Constitution was going to destroy the states.[20] The first words of the preamble alarmed Patrick Henry who wrote, "the question turns, Sir, on that poor little thing—the expression, *We, the people*, instead of the States of America."[21] The accusation that the federalists had "calculated ultimately to make the states one consolidated government"[22] was a frequent refrain reaching back to the earliest days of the Philadelphia Convention. The delegates had been gathered for less than a week and were still working it out amongst themselves about what they were hoping to accomplish, when the question was asked "whether [the new plan] was intended to annihilate State governments?"[23] The source of this concern was the cardinal fear of the new constitution: the size and great geographical and cultural heterogeneity of the nation was not conducive to being governed by a central authority.

James Winthrop of Massachusetts wrote of the differences between the North and the South that made it impossible for the national government to make policy for the nation (as well as foreshadowing the Civil War and the pretentious superiority toward the South that Northerners will embrace):

> The idle and dissolute inhabitants of the south, require a different regimen from the sober and active people of the north. . . . Many circumstances render us an essentially different people from the inhabitants of the southern states. The unequal distribution of property, the toleration of slavery, the ignorance and poverty of the lower classes, the softness of the climate, and dissoluteness of manners, mark their character. Among us, the care that is taken of education, small and nearly equal estates, equality of rights, and the severity of the climate, renders the people active, industrious and sober. Attention to religion and good morals is a distinguishing trait in our character. It is plain, therefore, that we require for our regulation laws, which will not suit the circumstances of our southern brethren, and the laws made for them would not apply to us.[24]

It was held that "the respective state governments must be the principal guardians of the people's rights."[25] As far as the antifederalists were concerned, the commonsense of this matter was settled and they reached back for support to Montesquieu, the man mentioned more than any other when it came to designing a Constitution:

> It is natural for a republic to have only a small territory; otherwise it cannot long subsist. In an extensive republic there are men of large fortunes, and consequently of less moderation; there are trusts too considerable to be placed in any single subject; he has interests of his own; he soon begins to think that he may be happy and glorious, by oppressing his fellow-citizens; and that he may raise himself to grandeur on the ruins of his country.
>
> In an extensive republic the public good is sacrificed to a thousand private views; it is subordinate to exceptions, and depends on accidents. In a small one, the interest of the public is more obvious, better understood, and more within the reach of every citizen; abuses have less extent, and, of course, are less protected.[26]

History had demonstrated what the ablest writers had expressed—only smaller states are capable of protecting freedom. "Large and consolidated empires may indeed dazzle the eyes of a distant spectator with their splendor, but if examined more nearly are always found to be full of misery" for the simple reason that "in large states the same principles of legislation will not apply to all parts.[27] The antifederalists did not accept the federalist's assurances that the states would retain significant authority and that the national government would be restricted to exercising only the delegated powers. They believed instead "that the direct tendency of the proposed system, is to consolidate the whole empire into one mass, and, like the tyrant's bed, to reduce all to one standard."[28]

THE FEDERALISTS

The federalists' position was that a more energetic national government was not to be feared. The chief difference between the antifederalists and the federalists might be captured in this one statement of Madison's that followed the famous "if men were angels" passage: "you must first enable government to control the governed; and in the next place oblige it to control itself."[29] The antifederalists believed that the new government would not control itself and would soon be crushing the liberties of the people. The supposed checks and balances would not work, the nation was on the road to despotism, and those who had deceptively created a new constitution had shown themselves to be men of low character.

To the contrary, argued Madison, there was less to worry about with the newly strengthened central authority than from the state governments. Anarchy under the current system was to be feared more than tyranny, for it is more likely that there will be continued defiance from the states.[30] Madison's loss of faith in the good behavior of state governments originated with his experiences during the Revolution. In letters to

Jefferson he had complained that the army was faced with the choice of disbanding or "living on free quarter." The treasury was empty, credit exhausted, and Congress lacked the ability to enforce any measures. They could only "[recommend] plans to the several states for execution" and wait for the states to separately "[rejudge] the expediency of such plans."[31] Some of the states were more shamefully deficient than others, and with the general government lacking power "the whole confederacy may be insulted and the most salutary measures frustrated by the most inconsiderable State in the Union."[32]

Alexander Hamilton, who had witnessed first-hand the deprivations that the army endured during the war, wrote that only a vigorous government could secure liberty and that the antifederalists who were objecting to the needed improvements in government were uninformed and short-sighted. He reminded his readers of the connection between safety, that only an active government can ensure, and liberty. "Vigor of government," wrote Hamilton, "is essential to the security of liberty." Despotism was more likely to result from too much enthusiasm for rights than for a "zeal for the firmness and efficiency of government."[33]

The federalists were contextualizing the problem of virtue in a new way. There existed a positive correlation between virtue and ability to rule, and it had become alarmingly apparent that nature had not been equitable in her distribution of that attribute. As Hamilton put it, people have a tendency to be "ambitious, vindictive, and rapacious."[34] For the benefit of the common welfare, certain features of the invigorated national government would result in the selection of leaders with greater wisdom and better qualifications than had been experienced in the state legislatures. Though Madison admitted that "enlightened statesmen will not always be at the helm,"[35] he expected to find more men of good character in the rarified offices of the national government, particularly in the senate and the presidency, than in the state legislatures. In addition, the method for determining who would serve would allow for increasing levels of detachment from, and thereby the ability to resist, the impulsive, ignorant, and leading-to-tyranny passions of the people.

First, the revised federal system was designed in such a way so that the virtuous few could be lifted above the hoi polloi in the states and granted greater authority in the national government. Second, through enlarging the sphere of government, the ability for the unvirtuous rabble to exert a harmful influence was limited. A sinister group might easily assume a majority in a state, but their influence will be checked as their views were refined by those serving in the national government. The influence of factious leaders and the poor decisions of the people will be diffused "by passing them through the medium of a chosen body of citizens, whose wisdom may best discern the true interest of their country."[36]

Federalist No.10 was Madison's first contribution to the collection of articles that were written to support ratification. He focused on the advantages of the extended republic over the many evils of smaller units of government where factions could tyrannize. Madison went beyond just doubting the ability of the people to directly self-govern. He claimed that it was unjust. In one magnificent dismissal of democracy, Madison wrote that no man should be able to judge what is best for himself because private interests distort judgment and integrity. Decision that have an immediate and personal impact must be lifted up and away from the people.[37]

The representatives in the national government would not be held captive to the selfish concerns of the people; it would become the safe harbor of virtue. The senators and the president served relatively longer terms than was typically allowed in the state constitutions—there were no term limits—and they were not dependent on the states for their pay. The representatives were given the time and distance that would allow them to take a more expansive view on what was fair and just. They would be impartial judges of what was good; not slaves to selfishness, passion, and impulse.

Happiness had been the goal that would lead to a harmonious community. Unfortunately, people in the states had proven to be self-indulgent and careless of the nation's collective welfare. Recall that virtue in the Aristotelian sense was the central pillar that the good life depended upon. Both sides of the ratification debate agreed that "free government can only exist where the body of the peoples are virtuous" wrote an antifederalist, because in such a government the people ultimately determine the condition of society.[38] The federalists' scathing evaluation of the behavior of the people in the sovereign states, however, indicated that the people were generally lacking in the most important virtues. They were not moderating their passions. They were dishonoring justice by disrespecting the laws and public welfare. They were not exercising wisdom when electing representatives and in passing laws.

Would virtue prevail in the national government? Hopefully yes; but there were mechanisms in place for when human nature faltered. When virtue failed, the human vices would ironically be what kept the system working as it should. In *Federalist No. 51* Madison wrote that the preservation of liberty was dependent upon the separation of powers. If virtue wavered, then the vice of personal ambition would prevent any one person or group to tyrannize. Madison believed that the great security against concentrated powers was the self-interest of each of the branches to retain power and resist encroachments.[39] Each branch would be so protective of its own prerogatives that it would block the expansion of power in the other branches. The power shared between the states and national government, and the checks and balances among the three branches, would allow for "ambition to counteract ambition."[40] Power was viewed as a zero-sum game. Each branch would be watchful for usurpations of power from one of the other departments.

In *Federalist No. 55* Madison appeared to be feeling a little more confident that virtue would prevail in the national government. He argued that the exaggerated fears that those vested with expanded authority in the new structure of government could easily abuse their power was unreasonable. He admitted that "there is a degree of depravity in mankind" but the belief in republican government was dependent on the belief that human nature consisted of other qualities "which justify a certain portion of esteem and confidence." If human nature was as unpredictable as the antifederalists had portrayed, and men were so completely devoid of virtue, then it must follow that self-government would never work. Only a despot could keep us from destroying one another.[41]

Perhaps in a move to ameliorate the defensiveness in the states caused by his earlier attacks, Madison wrote of the great genius that had been demonstrated by the American people. Responding to the concern that the representatives (sixty-five at the time of ratification) who would sit in the House could not be safely trusted with their delegated powers, he claimed to be unable to imagine that the American people would choose so large a number of men with low character who would be bent on a scheme of tyranny.[42] He reminded his readers of the virtue of the Continental Congress that had governed through the revolution. That governing body had been smaller in number, they operated in secret, the immediate fate of the nation was in their hands, yet the public trust was not betrayed and there were never even hints of corruption.[43]

The virtue of the common people became less important as it was assumed that a natural aristocracy would flourish, particularly in the senate and the presidency.[44] This was a model of leadership that was expressed in the legend of Cincinnatus, a virtuous leader who gave up the opportunity to be a dictator in order to return to modest life on the farm. Many of the founders' heroes had been Athenian aristocrats who had tried to contain the vices of the people. Solon, for example, was often praised by the founders as the model of wisdom and moderation. The most romanticized of all their heroes were Cato the Younger, Brutus, Cassius, and Cicero—all of whom were hero-worshiped for their selflessness and struggles to protect liberty.[45] The convention that produced the Constitution, Hamilton reminded the reader, was composed of men of unimpeachably good character. They "possessed the confidence of the people," reminded Hamilton, and they were known for their patriotism, virtue, and good judgment.[46]

A significant theme throughout the *Federalist Papers* was that the large nation would serve as an expanded pool of talent from which the central government would draw men of the highest caliber.[47] Numerous features within the Constitution would ensure that men of the highest caliber and integrity would be selected to serve. There were no religious or property qualifications, only merit will have distinguished them.[48] As Hamilton well knew from his own story, there are good minds to be found everywhere, and the best will rise to the top and be recognized.[49] The new constitution not only created a national government where the more virtuous leaders would be lifted above the common man, but as experience had demonstrated, the common man could be quite feckless and their voices needed to be muffled.

Because the senators would be selected by the state legislatures and not (as were members of the House of Representatives) by popular vote, it was expected that they would proceed with more coolness and wisdom. The use of the word "senate" as opposed to "congress" carried the connotation that this would be an assembly of aristocratic men. Fewer members in the Senate was also an advantage, for as you increase the number in any legislative body, "you communicate to them the vices which they are meant to correct . . . and the more they [partake] of the infirmities of their constituents."[50] It was assumed that the state legislatures would select the most eminent men to be senators who were recognized for their ability and virtue. With an age qualification of thirty-five, the senators would have had time to develop good judgment and come to understand the national interests.[51]

When it came to the selection of officers to serve on the Supreme Court, the method of appointment by the president and approval by the Senate assured that only the properly prepared would serve. It did not make sense that all officers in the government should be selected by the people at large, for they lacked the knowledge to make the best selections. In choosing people to serve in the judiciary branch this was of particular importance. The primary consideration was that only the people of good character with the best qualifications would be chosen to serve.[52]

In defending the method of appointment for the president, there was a particular effort made to assure that the vices of human nature could be circumvented. There would be no popular vote. State legislatures would select the men who would elect the president. The system of selecting the electors would ensure that the will of the people would be felt but that "tumult and disorder" would be avoided. The electors were detached from one another, would be selected to serve for this only one purpose, and therefore corruption and intrigue might safely be avoided.[53] It was predicted that this unique election process "affords a moral certainty, that the office of president will seldom fall to the lot of any man who is not in an eminent degree endowed with the requisite qualifications. . . . There will be a constant probability of seeing the station filled by characters preeminent for ability and virtue."[54] The president would enjoy a serene separation from the people and remain above any prevailing "ill-humors" in society. In *Federalist No. 71* Hamilton stressed how important it was for the president not to be influenced by "every sudden breeze of passion, or to every transient impulse" that may activate the people.[55]

On July 3, 1776, John Adams wrote to Abigail of his concerns that America will soon be facing "calamities" and "distresses" as the result of the break from England. He added, however, that trying times might have a good effect:

> It will inspire Us with many Virtues, which We have not, and correct many Errors, Follies, and Vices, which threaten to disturb, dishonor, and destroy Us. — The Furnace of Affliction produces Refinement, in States as well as Individuals. And the new Governments we are assuming, in every Part, will require a Purification from our Vices, and an Augmentation of our Virtues or there will be no Blessings. The People will have unbounded Power. And the People are extremely addicted to Corruption and Venality, as well as the Great.[56]

In 1776 Adams could only hope for the best. Although people were indeed prone to corruption, perhaps the trials of the coming years would be a character-building experience for the citizens and bring about an improvement in virtue. Eleven years after Adams wrote that letter to his wife, the hope that a republic of virtue would flourish had diminished. Virtue was not strong enough to inhibit the people from passing bad laws and impinging on the rights of others. A stronger national government would fill the void. It was hoped that the new system of checks and balances would prevent the newly increased powers in the national government from expanding. In addition, there was great faith that the qualifications for office and other structural processes would lead to the lifting up of the most virtuous into the offices of the national government.

The Constitution was ratified, however, by a narrow margin and only with the promise that it would be amended with provisions that would clarify the individual rights that Congress could not violate. This was an important shift toward the emphasis on individual rights rather than virtue. From 1789 forward, liberty was increasingly an issue of individual rights, devoid of any self-set limits emanating from a virtuous understanding of moral responsibility or concern for the public welfare when making choices. Rather than an expectation that personal liberty must be controlled by internal self-regulation, it was an experience that would be worked out between the individual and government.

The founders' understanding of liberty incorporated four important concepts: (1) personal liberty was a belief in individual rights, (2) political liberty was the right to participate in government, (3) internal liberty was the understanding that true freedom cannot exist without virtue, and (4) public good liberty expressed the understanding that all experiences are shaped by context, and freedom will only flourish within a community of citizens benevolently concerned with the common welfare. The vision was really not all that complex. American liberty would flourish through the efforts of virtuous citizens who honored good character and were concerned with the welfare of others. In the next chapter, I will look at how internal and public good liberty continued to decline as part of what liberty was meant to encompass.

NOTES

1. Benjamin Franklin, "Benjamin Franklin, To the Abbes Chalut and Arnoux, April 1787," *The Federalist Papers*, last modified December 2, 2012, accessed February 4, 2020, https://thefederalistpapers.org/founders/franklin/benjamin-franklinto-the-abbes-chalut-and-arnoux-april-1787.
2. Gordon S. Wood, *The Creation of the American Republic: 1776–1787* (Chapel Hill: University of North Carolina Press, 1998), 515.
3. Patrick Henry, "Speeches of Patrick Henry in the Virginia State Ratifying Convention, 5 June 1788," *The Anti-Federalist*, 310.
4. Ibid., 299.
5. Federal Farmer, "Letter I (October 8, 1787)," *The Anti-Federalist*, 35.
6. "The Address and Reasons of Dissent of the Minority of the Convention of Pennsylvania to Their Constituents (18 December 1787)," in *The Anti-Federalist*, 209.
7. Brutus, "To the Citizens of the State of New York, 1 November 1787," in *The Anti-Federalists*, 118–9.
8. Agrippa, "To the People of Massachusetts (27 November 1787)," in *The Anti-Federalist*, 232.
9. Federal Farmer, "Letter I (October 8, 1787)," in *The Anti-Federalist*, 36.
10. Ibid.
11. "The Address and Reasons of Dissent of the Minority of the Convention of Pennsylvania to Their Constituents (18 December 1787)," in *The Anti-Federalist*, 204.
12. Agrippa, "To the People (8 January 1788)," Letters of Agrippa, accessed January 28, 2018, http://www.constitution.org/afp/agrippa.htm.
13. "Centinel, Letter I (October 1787)," in *The Anti-Federalist*, 15.
14. Federal Farmer, "Letter IV (October 12, 1787)," in *The Anti-Federalist*, 56.
15. Federal Farmer, "Letter III (October 10, 1787)," in *The Anti-Federalist*, 49.
16. Agrippa, "To the People (23 November 1787)," in *The Anti-Federalist*, 230.
17. "Centinel, Letter I (October 1787)," in *The Anti-Federalist*, 17.
18. Ibid., 19.
19. Ibid., 16.
20. Herbert J. Storing, *The Anti-Federalist: Writings by the Opponents of the Constitution*, ed. Herbert J. Storing and Murray Dry (Chicago: University of Chicago Press, 1985), 227.
21. Patrick Henry, "Speeches of Patrick Henry in the Virginia State Ratifying Convention, 5 June 1788," in *The Anti-Federalist*, 297.
22. Federal Farmer, "Letter I (October 8, 1787)," in *The Anti-Federalist*, 37.
23. Robert Yates, "Notes of the Secret Debates of the Federal Convention of 1787, Taken by the Late Hon Robert Yates, Chief Justice of the State of New York, and One of the Delegates from That State to the Said Convention," The Avalon Project: Documents in Law, History, and Politics, accessed January 28, 2018, http://avalon.law.yale.edu/18th_century/yates.asp.
24. Agrippa, "Agrippa XII Part 1, To the Massachusetts Convention (January 11, 1788)," Teaching American History, accessed January 28, 2018, http://teachingamericanhistory.org/library/document/agrippa-xii/.
25. Federal Farmer, "Letter I (October 8, 1787)," in *The Anti-Federalist*, 38.
26. Charles Louis de Secondat de Montesquieu, *The Spirit of the Laws*, ed. Anne M. Cohler, Basia C. Miller, and Harold S. Stone (Cambridge: Cambridge University Press, 2009), 124.

27. Agrippa, "To the People (3 December 1787)," in *The Anti-Federalist*, 235.
28. Ibid., 236.
29. Madison, "No. 51," in *The Federalist*, 269.
30. James Madison, "Speech in the Federal Convention on the General and State Governments (June 21, 1787)," in *James Madison: Writings*, ed. Jack N. Rakove, 4th ed. (New York: Literary Classics of the United States, 2011), 108. Madison and Hamilton continued to make this point in *Federalist*, 17, 18, 19.
31. Madison, "To Thomas Jefferson (March 27, 1780)," in *James Madison: Writings*, 11.
32. Madison, "To Thomas Jefferson (April 16, 1780)," in *James Madison: Writings*, 13.
33. Hamilton, "No. 1," in *The Federalist*, 3.
34. Hamilton, "No. 6," in *The Federalist*, 21.
35. Madison, "No. 10," in *The Anti-Federalist*, 45.
36. Madison, "No. 10," in *The Anti-Federalist*, 46.
37. Ibid., 44.
38. "Centinel, Letter I (October 1787)," in *The Anti-Federalist*, 16.
39. Madison, "No. 51," in *The Federalist*, 268.
40. Ibid., 270.
41. Madison, "No. 55," in *The Federalist*, 291.
42. Ibid., 289.
43. Ibid., 290.
44. See David R. Weaver, "Leadership, Locke, and the Federalist," *American Journal of Political Science* 41, no. 2 (April 1997).
45. Carl J. Richard, *The Founders and the Classics: Greece, Rome, and the American Enlightenment* (Cambridge, MA: Harvard University Press, 1995), 55–57.
46. Hamilton, "No. 2," 7.
47. Jay, "No. 4," in *The Federalist*, 15.
48. Madison, "No. 57," in *The Federalist*, 296.
49. Hamilton, "No. 36," in *The Federalist*, 173.
50. James Madison, "Remarks in the Federal Convention on the Senate (June 7, 1787)," in *James Madison: Writings*, 98.
51. Jay, "No. 64," in *The Federalist*, 333.
52. Madison, "No. 51," in *The Federalist*, 268.
53. Hamilton, "No. 68," in *The Federalist*, 354.
54. Ibid., 354.
55. Hamilton, "No. 71," in *The Federalist*, 370.
56. John Adams, "Letter from John Adams to Abigail Adams (July 3, 1776)," Adams Family Papers, accessed February 1, 2018, https://www.masshist.org/digitaladams/archive/doc?id=L17760703ja.

NINE
Liberty

The Box with the False Bottom

Liberty is the cardinal value in American history. The praise for liberty has been a continuing tradition that reaches back to antiquity. It was Americanized by the Christianity of the seventeenth-century settlers, was elaborated upon by the Enlightenment context of the Revolution, and was documented as the nation's most important value in the Declaration of Independence and the preamble to the Constitution. The inheritance of liberty continues to be honored without understanding what it originally meant, or how much the meaning has changed. The four-note musical chord metaphorically captured the original understanding of liberty. Unfortunately, the tune has changed. Montesquieu wrote that "the corruption of each government almost always begins with that of its principles."[1] There was no principle more imperative to the founders than virtue; today virtue has become an anachronism—a fuddy-duddy sort of word.

Moral responsibility is no longer considered to be the foundation of good government. As a result, the lack of virtue in our political leaders is not a pressing concern. The value that was traditionally placed on virtue meant that the exercise of liberty carried important moral responsibilities for each individual citizen. This is no longer the case. Rather than virtue being the internalized and stabilizing force for good, the responsibility for maintaining the good life has been externalized and is now largely the responsibility of the national government. Virtue had placed internal limitations upon the exercise of liberty and established an agreed upon standard of the good life. The only true value that remains is an aggressively individualistic concern for rights.

Today's individualism has taken an ugly turn. Personal fulfillment has ceased to be inextricably connected with the well-being of the community. In the four-note chord of liberty, the individualism that underpinned personal liberty was balanced by a concerned involvement with the community. What it means to be connected to the community has fundamentally changed. The manner of relating to others through Facebook, Twitter, or Instagram (or whatever is the newest social media platform) is more about incessant self-defining than creating real communities. Researchers in the social sciences have looked at the growing problems of social isolation that are accentuated through social media.[2] In a recent meta-analysis, a strong connection was found between the use of social media, such as Facebook, and high levels of both loneliness and narcissism. A bidirectional relationship was suggested with the characteristics leading to greater use of social media, and the greater use causing higher levels of distress.[3] In the social media pseudo-community there is communication that not only lacks obligations of civility, but encourages offensiveness—the so-called social media disinhibition effect. The Aristotelian virtue of moderation is never rewarded in an environment where outrage, shock, novelty, and boundary pushing receives the most attention.

The need for virtue was important to the foundation narrative, and so it was perpetuated. Values shift, however, with historic context. To help explain how this happened in the United States, I will look to Alexis de Tocqueville's *Democracy in America*. In 1831 Tocqueville began a tour of the United States that was intended to be a study of the American prison system. Having lived through the trauma of the French Revolution, it was not unexpected that his interests would broaden to include observations concerning the American values of equality and liberty. Nearly two-hundred years after it was written, his book continues to be a marvelous source for insight on the unique features of early America. I will mine the text for his understanding of the vulnerabilities that faced this country. The potentialities that Tocqueville identified concur with my beliefs about what did in fact happen to liberty. Internal and public good liberty are no longer relevant to modern notions of liberty. Tocqueville described the possible unintended consequences of beliefs in freedom and equality. People can become less virtuous, more individualistic, distracted by material well-being, less concerned with good character and, quite frankly, too busy.

In an interesting digression on language, Tocqueville addressed a problem with words that is at the center of this project. Words can subtly shift their meaning without us being fully aware. He commented upon the vagueness of language that resulted from vacillating thoughts. He observed that men who live in democratic countries prefer to use words with unclear meanings because context continually shifts.[4] This is exactly what has been done to our most important word: liberty. Tocqueville wrote, "an abstract word is like a box with a false bottom; you put the ideas that you want into it, and you take them out without anyone seeing."[5]

The domino effect that America was susceptible to went as follows. Where there are no traditional aristocracies there is an elevation of a spirit of equality. This spirit of equality causes people to focus on their individuality rather than their class ties, and leads people to become more materialistic and isolated. Overtime these changes cause administrative centralization (a novel phrase coined by Tocqueville) and a loss of interest in local government. At the same time, industrialization leads to an array of new issues which also encourages the administrative centralization of power.

The tradition of hereditary aristocracy was never established in America, and according to Tocqueville, equality was the defining and most celebrated American value. It was certainly overstated.[6] Nonetheless, when compared to Europe, America was indeed the land of equality. Furthermore, American equality was not the result of a violent attack on tradition, as had happened so horrifically in France. Americans were born equal. Fifty years before Tocqueville's grand tour, Hector St. Jean de Crevecoeur wrote in 1782 of the spirit of equality that a European traveler would find when he visited America:

> It is not composed, as in Europe, of great lords who possess everything and of a herd of people who have nothing. Here are no aristocratical families, no courts, no kings, no bishops, no ecclesiastical dominion, no invisible power giving to a few a very visible one; no great manufacturers employing thousands, no great refinements of luxury. The rich and the poor are not so far removed from each other as they are in Europe . . . . We have no princes, for whom we toil, starve, and bleed: we are the most perfect society now existing in the world. Here man is free; as he ought to be; nor is this pleasing equality so transitory as many others are.[7]

There was a downside, however, to the loss of an entrenched class hierarchy and the expansion of equality. Equality made people focus on their individual independence and less on the welfare of others. Tocqueville observed that with the collapse of a system where people are bound by class ties, they become too self-interested.[8] Although there were certainly advantages to social mobility, it tended to lead to greater isolation and to an excessive love of material enjoyments.[9] Tocqueville described this dystopia of individualism where "every man is constantly spurred on by a desire to rise and a fear of falling." When money, rather than class identity, is what distinguishes one from another, and money fluctuates so easily, everyone is preoccupied by the need to acquire and retain it. It follows that "the ruling passions become a desire for wealth at all cost, a taste for business, a love of gain, and a liking for comfort and material pleasures."[10]

Another threat to America was a new type of centralization of power, what Tocqueville called "administrative centralization." Tocqueville described two types of centralization: governmental and administrative. The labels may sound similar but the differences between the two are extremely important. Governmental centralization was established by intent for the purposes of efficiency. Administrative centralization happened with fits and starts and without awareness of the long-term damages. The United States Constitution had established governmental centralization. The delegated powers to the national government dealt with relationships among the states, foreign affairs, and other issues that would be uniformly and efficiently handled at the national level. Administrative centralization occurred when certain local and unique concerns that should ideally be handled at the local level were taken up by the central power.[11] This form of centralization was to be avoided, wrote Tocqueville, because it "enervates" the people and diminished the spirit of citizenship.[12] No central power, regardless of how rational or competent, could be involved with all the details of life in a great nation. It was beyond human power.[13]

The gist of the antifederalists' objection to the Constitution had been their fear of administrative centralization. The federalists argued that the Constitution had only established governmental centralization. As both sides would have been pleased to hear, Tocqueville did not believe that administrative centralization existed in the United States in the 1830s.[14] The Constitution had established a system of administrative de-centralization that had reserved to the states all non-delegated powers. As the antifederalists had predicted, however, it was not going to last. The tendency was for the central government to gradually assume more and more administrative functions.

Tocqueville echoed the words of the antifederalists when he wrote that power in government will naturally expand and absorb more of the details of administration.[15] Tocqueville warned that once the slide into administrative centralization has begun, it cannot be reversed. Government becomes a "complicated machine" where "all the gears fit together and offer mutual support." No lawmaker would be able to reverse the process "because he cannot remove one piece of the mechanism without disrupting the whole thing."[16] Administrative centralization threatened to change the very nature of the citizens, for above them would stand an enormous and unmanageable authority (what future generations would refer to as the "nanny state"). Tocqueville wrote of this tutelary power:

> Which takes upon itself alone to secure [the people's] gratifications and to watch over their fate. . . . It would be like the authority of a parent if, like that authority, its object was to prepare men for manhood; but it

seeks, on the contrary, to keep them in perpetual childhood. . . . For their happiness such a government willingly labors, but it chooses to be the sole agent and the only arbiter of that happiness; it provides for their security, foresees and supplies their necessities, facilitates their pleasures, manages their principal concerns, directs their industry, regulates the descent of property, and subdivides their inheritances: what remains, but to spare them all the care of thinking and all the trouble of living?[17]

Industrialization would also contribute to the rise of administrative centralization as well as a new type of aristocratic elite that would dominate society.[18] The agitations and fluctuations of the business cycle made wealth and status insecure, and caused people to fear disorder. They would increasingly look to the government to maintain law and order. Public tranquility is then valued above all else and becomes the only thing people really care much about. Citizens gradually allow the central power to assume more authority, for only it has the means to defend against anarchy.[19]

With the rise of industrial capitalism came the growth of a materialistic and competitive culture. The new aristocracy of wealth and power would be more harmful to the public good, thought Tocqueville, than the hereditary aristocracies of old for it lacked permanent class bonds. Marketplace fluctuations can make today's rich tomorrow's poor. The elements that form the class of the rich are not fixed by birth and tradition. Lacking permanent connections, they will not exert the benevolent influence over society that had been expected of the old aristocracy. The ascendant manufacturing aristocracy was one of the harshest that has appeared on the earth, observed Tocqueville, due to the fact that they lacked compassion for the misery of the workers.

Tocqueville did not believe that the United States was necessarily headed in this dire direction of self-absorbed individualism, crass materialism, and massive administrative centralization; his primary goal had been to heighten the awareness and thereby combat them.[20] He had come to America in order to study the best example of what he believed to be a worldwide historic trend: the expansion of democracy. Perhaps America's long tradition of liberty, the guarantees in the Bill of Rights, the federal system that left significant authority at the local level, and proper moral values, would prevent the fall. He was wrong on two counts: (1) he misjudged the sustaining power of virtue, and (2) he did not predict the loss of the power of state governments.

Shared principles keep a country strong and united. As Tocqueville wrote, "for society to exist . . . citizens must always be brought and held together by some principled ideas; and that cannot happen without each one of them coming at times to draw his opinions from the same source and consenting to receive a certain number of ready-made beliefs."[21] The most important ready-made belief was the importance of virtue—what Tocqueville called *mores*.

Through the influence of Christianity moral standards had been deeply woven into the American way of life. If Americans hoped to obtain "the happy fruits that they expect," they must realize that it would only come from "morality, spirituality, [and] belief."[22] Tocqueville used the word "mores" as a synonym for virtue. Mores were an "ensemble of ideas . . . the whole of the dispositions that man brings to the government of society . . . enlightenment, habits, knowledge."[23] He considered them to be vital, as did the founders, to the maintenance of the freedom and equality that he observed in America. The earliest title that Tocqueville proposed for his book, *American Institutions and Mores*,[24] expressed his theory that the religious mores of the American people were of central importance to the stability that he observed in the 1830s.[25]

It was not the specific doctrines and dogmas associated with religion, but the way all Christian religions influenced moral behavior and prevented licentiousness. Tocqueville's statements about the importance of religious mores was what the founders meant when they stressed the significance of virtue. Despotism did not need religion; liberty could not do without it.[26] Christianity was fundamentally important because it taught Americans "the art of being free."[27] The capacity for liberty was the ability to moderate destructive passions and understand our duties to one another. The political arrangements in America may have been what gave the citizens their taste for liberty, but it was Christianity that "singularly facilitates their use of it."[28]

The other factor Tocqueville identified that could prevent the destructive growth of excessive individualism was the way the Americans had constructed their political system. The Constitution had created a federal system that left significant authority to local government. The activities of the national government fostered little unity in that only the "principal citizens" gathered at one place for brief periods, and no lasting bonds would be established.[29] Citizens maintain only a very limited interest in national affairs because they tend not to have an immediately perceivable impact on everyday life. Local government, on the other hand, fostered relationships and concern for the public good. Political liberty when exercised at the level of the immediate community "make a great number of citizens put value on the affection of their neighbors and of those nearby, constantly bring men back toward each other despite their instincts that separate them."[30]

Local government would not only foster the benevolent interest in the public good, but would in turn promote virtue in the citizenry that was otherwise undermined by individualism. If not redirected toward a concern for the welfare of the community, individualism collapsed into egoism, and "egoism parches the seed of all virtues."[31] Concern for others was the cultivator of virtue "it forms a multitude of steady, temperate, moderate, farsighted citizens who have self-control; and if it does not lead directly to virtue by will, it imperceptibly draws closer to virtue by habits."[32]

Tocqueville hoped that continued direct involvement in local government, that had been symbolized by the New England townhall, would prevent the establishment of a monolithic central authority. As individualism increased, however, citizens would find it increasingly difficult to pull away from their private concerns and pay attention to public affairs.[33] Furthermore, people can become just too busy to pay much attention. Private life can be "so agitated, so full of desires, of work, that hardly any energy or leisure is left to any man for political life."[34]

Unfortunately, federalism as originally designed no longer exists in the United States. The federal system has evolved, as all systems will do. Our federal system was intended to operate in such a way that power would be divided between the states' and the national government. The powers delegated to the national government were to be limited to those enumerated in the Constitution. The federal system that was established in 1789 was not meant to improperly dominate the states. Madison had promised in *Federalist No. 46* that all domestic and personal interests of the people will be handled by the state governments. Today, from the relatively non-contentious question of determining the legal drinking age, to the most incendiary moral problems of abortion and gay marriage, to the major public policy debates over mandatory health insurance and education, the ultimate course of action has been determined by the national government. The Constitution lists none of these as delegated areas of concern for the executive or legislative branches. As the antifederalists in the 1780s, and Tocqueville fifty years later had argued, it was a fundamental truth that any central power would naturally tend to take on more power.

In addition to the enlargement of the federal government, the power of the presidency has been outrageously inflated beyond anything the founders had in mind. Terms such as the "imperial presidency" and the "bully pulpit" are routinely applied to the chief executive. The only reference Tocqueville made to Andrew Jackson, the president who was serving at the time of his visit, was to dismissively wonder about how the people could have elected "a man of violent character and middling capacity; nothing in all the course of his career had ever proved that he had the qualities necessary to govern" and to whom "the enlightened classes had always been opposed." His explanation was that the people had just been too impressed by an inconsequential event (i.e., the 1815 Battle of New Orleans).[35]

One of the key parts of the Constitution, as understood by Tocqueville, was the weakness of the presidency. It was therefore an interesting omission that he did not reflect on the power-extending and Constitution-violating tendencies of the men who had held the office in the first decades since ratification.[36] Tocqueville argued that the tendency would be for the legislative branch to expand its power.[37] The office of the presidency would remain relatively quiet because the executive did not make or propose laws.[38] He viewed the presidency, when compared to the legislature, "as an inferior and dependent power."[39] He may prepare treaties or designate officers for government, but they must be approved by the legislature, he is the head of the army and navy, but they are inconsequentially small.[40] When Tocqueville wrote that in "America, the President cannot stop the making of laws; he cannot escape the obligation to execute them . . . his support is undoubtedly useful, but it is not necessary,"[41] he lacked the prescience to see a future where presidents would not be reluctant to use their veto power, would carry out undeclared wars, and would rule through executive orders.

Tocqueville did predict that if the power of the central authority were to grow, that was when the power of the presidency could become dangerous. As the powers of the presidency increased, so would the inherent dangers of the elective system. The greater the power, wrote Tocqueville, the more "the ambition of the pretenders is excited, the more it finds support among a host of men of lesser ambition who hope to share power after their candidate has triumphed."[42] Limited power encouraged moderation; expanded power fueled passion. "Political passions become irresistible, not only because the objective that they pursue is immense, but also because millions of men experience those political passions in the same way and at the same moment . . . nothing is so contrary to the well-being and to the liberty of men."[43]

An important reason for the expansion of the national government—Tocqueville's administrative centralization—was the problem of virtue and the exercise of liberty. Virtue ceased to be important to liberty because it never really worked. The first acknowledgement of that fact had been with the writing of the Constitution. Since then, the nation has faced a number of crisis points that could not be solved because there were no shared principles that united the citizens. The major conflicts were: ending slavery, reining in unfettered capitalism, implementing measures to alleviate the Great Depression, and expanding civil rights in the 1950s.

There has been no crisis that was resolved through an expansion of state authority at the expense of the national. Citizens proclaiming liberty and operating on their own or through their state governments, could not agree on what the correct and moral choice must be. With each of these watershed events, the use of the word liberty was stretched and distorted. Liberty became more about individual rights and less about ethical responsibility. Shared principles of morality, a common vision of the good life, an understanding of the importance of moderation in all things, were ideas that slowly vanished from "the box with the false bottom." The national government slowly became the arbiter of the good life.

The beginning of the end for the style of federalism that the founders had designed was the Civil War. With the growth of abolitionism, by the mid-nineteenth century it had become too difficult to sustain the travesty that a nation established on principles of equality and liberty would continue to countenance slavery. It has been repeated so often that it has become historic doctrine, that the founders had no choice but to allow slavery for the sake of unity. That is assuming that we know the answer to the counter factual event. We do not know what would have happened if the founders had possessed the Aristotelian virtue of courage to have done what they knew was morally correct.[44]

By 1860, slavery could no longer remain a state issue. The South seceded, a war was fought, and the slaves were freed. "Cannon conquer, but they do not necessarily convert,"[45] stated the plain truth in an 1865 newspaper, and at the end of the war southern state legislatures worked to undermine the liberty of the freed slaves. Congress responded with an extraordinary level of intervention in the domestic affairs of the southern states. The Freedmen's Bureau, established in 1865 under the jurisdiction of the War Department, was the first welfare agency funded by the national government. Nowhere in Article I of the Constitution can even the loosest of constructionists find the delegated authority for Congress to establish hospitals and schools, oversee marriage and employment contracts, and provide food, shelter, and clothing to the destitute.

When the Civil War culminated in the end of slavery, Lincoln promised "a new birth of freedom." This renewed commitment to freedom became part of the Constitution with the Thirteenth Amendment that ended slavery. This was the first time that the Constitution was used to specifically restrict the liberty of one group (slaveholders) in order to promote the freedom for another. All of the previous amendments had been written to restrict the powers of the national government. The operative phrase being: "Congress shall make no law." The need to explicitly state the activities that Congress shall not do implied an inherent tension between the freedom loving good citizens and a potentially freedom destroying bad government. In the Thirteenth, Fourteenth, and Fifteenth Amendments—collectively known as the Reconstruction Amendments— there appeared a startlingly new phrase: "Congress shall have power." Congress assumed the power to make the citizens do the right thing.

The free enterprise system harmonized with the belief in personal liberty, but not with the tradition of virtuous moderation or concern with the common welfare. By the late nineteenth-century the people of this nation witnessed how freedom for industrialists resulted in brutal class conflict, increasing inequality, and fundamental threats to democracy with the accumulation of wealth among the politically powerful. Once again, the national debate focused on the central value of freedom. The power to oppress that resulted from too much money in too few hands led to the Progressive Era. Another property and freedom limiting amendment was added to the Constitution. The Sixteenth Amendment—the income tax—was a response to the concern that the wealthiest Americans had consolidated too much power. The expansion of the power of the national government to restrict capitalism continued through the nineteenth and twentieth centuries with the loosening of the interpretation of the commerce clause.

This redefining and restructuring of the power of the national government has continued under every administration, regardless of political party. Franklin Roosevelt's solution to the Great Depression called for more business regulation and central economic planning. Most important, he promoted a new value concept that was captured by the phrase "positive freedom." The Constitution was not amended, but the Supreme Court eventually altered their interpretation of the document to allow such government expanding legislation as Social Security. Franklin Roosevelt was the early architect of the welfare state and every president since has known better than to try to dismantle it. In 1954 the Supreme Court told the southern states to desegregate their schools, they resisted, and President Eisenhower sent in the Eighty-Second Airborne to force the citizens to be good. Today it is simply expected that problems will be met by assertive policy from the national government led by a president who will not be limited by a "parchment barrier."

NOTES

1. Charles Louis de Secondat de Montesquieu, *The Spirit of the Laws*, ed. Anne M. Cohler, Basia C. Miller, and Harold S. Stone, nachdr. ed. (Cambridge: Cambridge University Press, 2009), 112.
2. See for example Sherry Turkle, *Alone Together: Why We Expect More from Technology and Less from Each Other* (New York: Basic Books, 2001).
3. Dong Liu and Roy F. Baumeister, "Social Networking Online and Personality of Self-Worth: A Meta-Analysis," *Journal of Research and Personality* 64 (October 2016).
4. Tocqueville, "Part I, Chapter 16," 2:829.
5. Ibid.
6. See Carla Gardina Pestana and Sharon V. Salinger, eds., *Inequality in Early America* (Hanover, NH: University Press of New England, 1999).
7. Hector St. Jean de Crevecoeur, "Letters from an American Farmer (1782)," Digital History, accessed February 9, 2018, http://www.digitalhistory.uh.edu/disp_textbook.cfm?smtid=3&psid=3644.
8. Alexis de Tocqueville, *The Old Regime and the Revolution*, trans. John Bonner (New York: Harper and Brothers, 1856), ix–xi, accessed February 9, 2018, http://oll.libertyfund.org/titles/2419.
9. Tocqueville, "Part I, Chapter 5," *Democracy*, 2:745.
10. Tocqueville, *The Old Regime*, ix–xi.
11. Tocqueville, "Part I, Chapter 5," *Democracy*, 1:143.
12. Ibid., 1:147.
13. Ibid., 1:154.
14. Ibid., 1:147.
15. Ibid., 1:163.
16. Ibid., 1:148.

17. Ibid., "Part IV, Chapter 6," 2:1250.
18. In 1790 John Adams wrote that this nation would never be a true republic because *"alieni appetens sui profusus* (covetous of the property of others and prodigal of his own) reigns in this nation as a Body more than any other I have ever seen." John Adams, *John Adams: Writings from the New Nation 1784–1826*, ed. Gordon S. Wood (New York: Library of America, 2011), 244.
19. Tocqueville, "Part II, Chapter 20," 2:983.
20. Ibid., "Part IV, Chapter 3," 2:1201.
21. Ibid., "Part I, Chapter 2," 2:713.
22. Ibid., "Foreword," 2:693, note f.
23. Ibid., "Part I, Chapter 9," *Democracy*, 1:466
24. Eduardo Nolla, introduction to *Democracy in America*, 1: lxxxviii.
25. Tocqueville, "Part I, Chapter 9," *Democracy*, 1:466
26. Ibid., 1:467.
27. Ibid., 1:472.
28. Ibid., 1:475.
29. Ibid.
30. Ibid., "Part II, Chapter 4," *Democracy*, 2:892.
31. Ibid., "Part II, Chapter 2," 2:882.
32. Ibid., "Part II, Chapter 8," 2:922.
33. Ibid., "Part IV, Chapter 3," 2:1201.
34. Ibid.
35. Tocqueville, "Part II, Chapter 9," in *Democracy in America*, 1:453.
36. A few examples may suffice. John Adams fought an undeclared war with France and signed the First Amendment violating Alien and Sedition Acts. Thomas Jefferson believed that the Louisiana Purchase was unconstitutional, but thought it too important to turn down. Jefferson, supported by Madison, greatly expanded the national authority with the passage of the Embargo of 1807. John Quincy Adams supported a nationalistic and Constitution stretching program of internal improvements, the advancement of science, and the establishment of a national university.
37. Tocqueville, "Part I, Chapter 8," in Democracy, 1:202.
38. Ibid., 1:206.
39. Ibid., 1:207.
40. Ibid., 1:209.
41. Ibid., 1:210.
42. Ibid., 1:211.
43. Ibid., 1:258.
44. George Mason: "The augmentation of slaves weakens the states; and such a trade is diabolical in itself, and disgraceful to mankind"; Patrick Henry: "I believe a time will come when an opportunity will be offered to abolish this lamentable evil"; Thomas Jefferson: "Nothing is more certainly written in the book of fate than that these people are to be free"; George Washington: "There is not a man living who wishes more sincerely than I do, to see a plan adopted for the abolition of it"; John Adams: I have, throughout my whole life, held the practice of slavery in . . . abhorrence"; John Jay: "The honor of the States, as well as justice and humanity, in my opinion, loudly call upon them to emancipate these unhappy people." See Walter E. Williams, ed., "What the Founders Said about Slavery," Quotations from Framers of the Constitution and Others, last modified July 2, 2015, accessed February 7, 2018, http://econfaculty.gmu.edu/wew/quotes/slavery.html.
45. "What Next? Harper's Weekly, April 22, 1865, (Editorial)," Harpweek, accessed March 9, 2018, http://education.harpweek.com/TheReconstructionConvention/TheBeliefs/Belief7/Belief7-r003.htm.

Conclusion

Mourning Virtue

Liberty is fragile; it is forever the potential victim of power. In the preceding chapters the two sources of this power were investigated. One was interior: the power of the emotions and the lower drives that cause a person to make bad choices and undermine the good life. The great philosophers from antiquity addressed this, and I have looked at how two of the founding fathers, Jefferson and Franklin, dealt with it in their own lives. The other slayer of liberty was external: one of the three types of government—democracy, aristocracy, or monarchy—could collapse into a liberty-destroying tyranny. The early years of this nation's history was dominated by the struggle over how to structure a government that would stabilize the republic yet protect liberty. The first attempt failed. In 1789 the people ratified a new constitution that established a federal style of government with the central powers greatly increased.

The antifederalists, convinced that the power in the national government would continue to grow at the expense of the states, worried that this was the first step toward a liberty crushing centralization of power. They were right in that the momentum that began during the Philadelphia Convention to move power away from the states and toward the central authority continued. They had argued that it was an inherent fallacy to think that the system of checks and balances would limit the growth of power. They correctly predicted that the national government would take an elastic view of the delegated powers and the necessary and proper clause. The federalists, on the other hand, believed that the Constitution would save the floundering republic.

Neither side in the Constitutional debate foresaw the most profound change that the future would bring: a radical change in what it meant to be free. It was the genius of Tocqueville who understood the complex process that would result from the gradual centralization of power, the growth of a wealthy elite, the loss of concern for virtue, the overvaluing of individualism, and an apathy toward government. C. S. Lewis was right about the key to history: "Terrific energy is expended—civilizations are built up—excellent institutions devised; but each time something goes wrong."[1]

As the previous chapters have explained, the founders were not confused about what freedom should lead to or the definition of the good life. It was explicitly tied to a virtuous life. This is no longer true. Individualism has become the foremost American value. Two important books that resulted from thousands of interviews examined this new type of individualism and its impact. In *Habits of the Heart*, first published over twenty years ago, Robert Bellah and a team of researchers presented evidence accumulated after five years and over two hundred in-depth interviews. The title of the book is from Tocqueville who investigated the habits of the American character that would sustain liberty. Bellah's research supported the concerns that had worried Tocqueville about the undesirable potentialities of democracy. America might lose its strong moral tradition. Individualism would increase, people would withdraw into themselves and be disconnected from and uninterested in the larger community beyond their immediate family and closest friends. After interviewing thousands of Americans, Robert Putnam came to the same conclusion. The witty title of his book, *Bowling Alone*, came from the fact that although more people are bowling than ever before, there are fewer bowling leagues. Putnam believed this was symptomatic of a growing loss of interest in social connections.

Bellah found a general agreement over what freedom meant to the people he interviewed: "being left alone by others, not having other people's values, ideas, or styles of life forced upon one, being free of arbitrary authority in work, family, and political life."[2] The values of initiative, independence, and success were prioritized, but according to Bellah, people had forgotten that "freedom lies not in rejecting our social nature."[3] Although people seemed to have no problem articulating the importance of personal freedom, they tended to lack a vocabulary for what they should be accomplishing with their freedom. Bellah observed, "parents advocate 'values' for their children even when they do not know what those 'values' are."[4]

There was something arbitrary and diffuse about what defined the good life; there was no "common conception of the ends of a good life or ways to coordinate cooperative action with others."[5] A good life was where you set your own goals according to your own self-set priorities. That was where the confusion often began. There was a lack of clarity about the value to be placed on any set of priorities, and they could fluctuate according to how a person was feeling at any one moment according to a great variety of life circumstances. Bellah concluded that many Americans found themselves in an "inarticulate search" for any values that should serve as guidelines or a "vision of a good life or a good society." The commitment to freedom was "strangely without content."[6]

Putnam's research confirmed Bellah's. A majority of Americans believed that selfishness was a serious problem and that the country was on the wrong track morally and culturally.[7] With the ultimate value placed on the individual, the meaning of life was now found through private experience. The "touchstone of truth and goodness" was "individual experience and intimate relationships."[8] The impact of the demise of the community was the topic that interested Putnam. He investigated a concept called "social capital." The core idea being that dense social networks that involve reciprocity and trust contribute to productivity.[9]

From the Aristotelian perspective, the acquisition of virtue was what defined the good life for the individual. However, many of the virtues, such as truthfulness, generosity, even-temperedness, friendliness, and modesty are exercised within a social context. These virtues made for a better person, but they also were the foundation that hold social networks together. Research has demonstrated that when people believe that others are virtuous, they are more likely to behave virtuously themselves.[10] Social trust is the simple expectation that others will be good. In studies that compared social trust over the past decades, evidence seems to indicate that it has been falling since the 1960s.[11]

Virtue, as Aristotle had taught, required a constancy of effort. In *Democracy in America* there was a suggestion of a possible future state where citizens were isolated, worried about their financial well-being, disengaged from politics, and much too distracted. Who would have the time or energy to care about virtue? One of the factors that Tocqueville believed would contribute to a disconnect from the community was that changes in the market economy would make everyone just too busy. Indeed, it does appear that if there is any one value that Americans care about today it is busyness. We worship a cult of busyness. Putnam reported on how many people report feeling continually hurried. "I don't have enough time" is the major reason people give for not participating in community activities.[12] A 2015 analysis by the Gallup organization supported Putnam's research. For the past fourteen years, roughly 48 percent of Americans say they do not have enough time.[13]

Research published in *The Harvard Business Review* explored the changing value placed on being busy, from Thorstein Veblen's late nineteenth-century perspective on leisure as a status symbol to the present-day busyness as a status symbol. They reported on the dramatic increase of references to having "crazy schedules" in holiday letters since the 1960s. The overworked lifestyle has become associated with other valuable characteristics such as competence and ambition. Busyness has become the modern version of conspicuous consumption with celebrities associating their popularity with "having no life" in their Twitter humblebrags.[14] Certainly, mid-twentieth century Americans seemed not to have worried too much about hectic schedules. In one of the more interesting examples of side-tracked anxiety during a time of heightened concern over nuclear annihilation, Putnam cited a 1958 study which concluded that "the most dangerous threat hanging over American society is the threat of [too much] leisure."[15]

The obligation to be busy has replaced the obligation to be good. The Declaration's long list of grievances against King George concluded with the assertion that the character of the man made him "unfit to be the ruler of a free people." A leader lacking in virtue was not to be tolerated. Then again, if the people were lacking in virtue, would good character in the leader matter? Furthermore, does the lack of virtue in the community have an effect on how people report their overall satisfaction with life? If the answer to the above two questions is "no," that would surely be indicative of how virtue has ceased to be an issue of concern. Findings from a 2018 Gallup poll provided some evidence that perhaps that may be true. Only 28 percent of Americans reported that they were "very or somewhat satisfied" with the moral and ethical climate of the country.[16] Yet a solid 80 agreed that they were reasonably satisfied with the overall quality of their own life.

Here are a few other poll numbers to consider. In a 2017 poll, only 36 percent of Americans believed that President Trump was honest or trustworthy.[17] This was not simply a rebuke to Trump, for honesty does not appear to have been of any great importance when it came to the presidency in 2016. Although Hilary Clinton won the popular vote, just days before the election only 38 percent of voters believed that Hilary Clinton was more honest and trustworthy than Trump.[18] Both Trump and Clinton saw the highest unfavorable ratings since polling began in 1956. Juxtapose those numbers with the myth that American children grow up believing about George Washington: Washington confessed to cutting down the cherry tree because he could not tell a lie.

The story of the cherry tree was fictional; the message that Washington believed in the paramountcy of virtue was true. At the age of sixteen Washington wrote out a copy of *110 Rules of Civility*. It was more than a mere exercise in good penmanship, but was formative in the development of his views about good character that emphasized respect toward others, moderation in demeanor, and to always aim for reason over passion.[19] A little over forty years later in his first inaugural address, Washington remained consistent with those themes when he spoke of what his generation expected to be the essence of liberty:

> The foundations of our National policy will be laid in the pure and immutable principles of private morality . . . there is no truth more thoroughly established, than that there exists in the economy and course of nature, an indissoluble union between virtue and happiness, between duty and advantage.[20]

Jefferson believed that the success of the republic and the protection of liberty was dependent upon an educated population's active participation in government. According to voter statistics liberty is in trouble. In a recent survey, only 36 percent of respondents could name all three branches of government, 35 percent could not name a single one.[21] In a 2017 survey only 37 percent could name their district's member in the House of Representatives, although a little over half could name the party affiliation.[22] Turnout in presidential elections hovers between 50 and 60 percent and between 35 and 45 percent for midterm elections. Over 26 percent of males between the ages of eighteen and twenty-four are not even registered. It is clear that politics is hardly the national past-time.[23]

The United States was founded on an accepted truth: citizens have an unalienable right to liberty. This project explored the network of ideas that the founders meant to communicate when they recognized liberty as the human value upon which the new nation would be based. In the four-note chord of liberty there was harmony among four important ideas. Citizens must be free to make personal choices within the rule of law and be participants in the making of those laws. Both of those freedoms would contribute to the stability of the republic if the people understood the importance of virtue and were benevolently concerned with the well-being of others. Good character mattered.

These four ideas that were central to the concept of liberty were the means to the end of the ultimate human value: happiness. Too much has been removed from the happiness construct. Happiness was not a blissful state of smiling cheerfulness. It was a life based on self-knowledge, virtue, and shared community values. Whether learned from Aristotle, Cicero's speeches, Franklin's aphorisms, or so many other sources; honorable people would seek to cultivate truthfulness, good fellowship, nobility of spirit, and proper decorum. This was happiness.

Tocqueville pointed out that an abstract word is "like a box with a false bottom." We do not always fully understand what is in the box at any one time or what is being taken out. The most important concept that has been removed from the box is that virtue must set the boundaries around rights. There was an art to being free that was based on moral values. Without this expectation, the ever-lengthening list of rights (i.e., college education, internet access,) becomes just an empty demand for "more" without a reciprocal understanding of obligations. The current debate over a right to healthcare, for example, is devoid of any discussion of the recipient's obligations to make healthy lifestyle choices. According to current understanding, we have a right to not be judged for our choices. The philosophers from antiquity knew, however, that the ability to make good choices came from the acquisition of virtue. Christian traditions refocused this as a personal choice to follow the moral teachings of the Bible.

In 1944 Franklin Roosevelt was looking at the post-war world and envisioned a new era of national unity, comfort, and security for all Americans. "We cannot be content," spoke Roosevelt in his State of the Union Address, "if some fraction of our people—whether it be one-third or one-fifth or one-tenth- is ill-fed, ill-clothed, ill housed, and insecure." The first Bill of Rights was there to guard the liberties of the citizens. Government encroachment had been the concern. Roosevelt believed the time had come for a second Bill of Rights for the American people.

Government should guarantee to the citizens the kind of life needed in order to enjoy freedom.

> The right to a useful and remunerative job in the industries or shops or farms or mines of the Nation;
> The right to earn enough to provide adequate food and clothing and recreation;
> The right of every farmer to raise and sell his products at a return which will give him and his family a decent living;
> The right of every businessman, large and small, to trade in an atmosphere of freedom from unfair competition and domination by monopolies at home or abroad;
> The right of every family to a decent home;
> The right to adequate medical care and the opportunity to achieve and enjoy good health;
> The right to adequate protection from the economic fears of old age, sickness, accident, and unemployment;
> The right to a good education.[24]

Congress never passed this second Bill of Rights, but the expectation that citizens have these rights, that they define the good life, and that the government is responsible for ensuring them, has permeated society. The course of history has proven what Isaiah Berlin wrote:

> To offer political rights, or safeguards against intervention by the state, to men who are half-naked, illiterate, underfed, and diseased is to mock their condition: they need medical help or education before they can understand, or make use of an increase in their freedom. What is freedom to those who cannot make use of it? . . . individual freedom is not everyone's primary need.[25]

There is no doubt that the modern globalized economy has made life too complex for all to achieve the good life through mere application of individual effort. From the earliest years of American settlement, the importance of community was emphasized. As the first settlers knew and the founders believed, the good life was experienced in a social context. This 1630 inspirational speech from John Winthrop expressed the essence of Roosevelts' 1944 vision for the post-war nation application of effort to be virtuous (spelling has been modernized):

> We must be knit together in this work as one man, we must entertain each other in brotherly Affection, we must be willing to abridge ourselves of our superfluities, for the supply of others necessities, we must uphold a familiar Commerce together in all meekness, gentleness, patience and liberality, we must delight in each other, make others Conditions our own rejoice together, mourn together, labor, and suffer together, always having before our eyes our Commission and Commu-

nity in the work, our Community as members of the same body, so shall we keep the unity of the spirit in the bond of peace.[26]

The significant difference between Winthrop and Roosevelt's idealistic hope for the community was that for Roosevelt the responsibility shifted to the government.

The founders knew that liberty was destroyed externally by excessive power in the government, or internally by a lack of virtue. Today the modern understanding of liberty is not only commensurate with a powerful centralized authority, but is perceived as a necessity. As the Federalist writers were aware, the lack of virtue in the citizenry had not been sufficient. James Madison expressed the hope that virtue would continue to be a quality that we would find in our national leaders, particularly in the senate and the presidency. Events would indicate that virtue and the importance of good character has been removed from the "box with the false bottom." We do not appear to mourn the loss.

NOTES

1. C. S. Lewis, *Mere Christianity: A Revised and Amplified Edition, with a New Introduction, of the Three Books Broadcast Talks, Christian Behaviour, and beyond Personality*, fiftieth anniversary ed.; C. S. Lewis Signature Classics ed. (London: HarperCollins Publishers, 2002), 50.
2. Robert Neelly Bellah et al., *Habits of the Heart: Individualism and Commitment in American Life*, updated ed. (Berkeley: University of California Press, 2008), 23.
3. Ibid., xv.
4. Ibid., 144.
5. Ibid., 24.
6. Ibid., 25.
7. Robert D. Putnam, *Bowling Alone: The Collapse and Revival of American Community*, nachdr. ed. (New York, NY: Simon & Schuster, 2007), 25.
8. Bellah, *Habits of the Heart*, 143.
9. Putnam, *Bowling Alone*, 19.
10. Ibid., 137.
11. Ibid., 141–42.
12. Putnam, *Bowling Alone*, 189.
13. "Americans' Perceived Time Crunch No Worse than in Past," last modified December 31, 2015, accessed February 11, 2018, http://news.gallup.com/poll/187982/americans-perceived-time-crunch-no-worse-past.aspx.
14. Silvia Bellezza, Neeru Paharia, and Anat Keinan, "Research: Why Americans Are So Impressed by Busyness," *Harvard Business Review*, last modified December 15, 2016, accessed February 11, 2018, https://hbr.org/2016/12/research-why-americans-are-so-impressed-by-busyness.
15. Putnam, *Bowling Alone*, 16.
16. "Political Splits Widen on Satisfaction with Life in U.S.," Gallup, last modified January 25, 2018, accessed February 6, 2018, http://news.gallup.com/poll/226211/political-splits-widen-satisfaction-life.aspx?g_source=CATEGORY_WELLBEING&g_medium=topic&g_campaign=tiles. There was an interesting flip between Democrats and Republicans between 2017 and 2018 when asked about whether they were satisfied with the overall quality of life 2017: 85 percent of Democrats agreed and 74 percent of Republican agreed; 2018: 76 percent of Democrats agreed and 90 percent of Republicans agreed.

17. "Majority in U.S. No Longer Thinks Trump Keeps His Promises," Gallup, last modified April 17, 2017, accessed February 7, 2018, http://news.gallup.com/poll/208640/majority-no-longer-thinks-trump-keeps-promises.aspx.

18. Scott Clement and Emily Guskin, "Post-ABC Tracking Poll Finds Race Tied, as Trump Opens Up an 8-Point Edge on Honesty," *Washington Post*, last modified November 2, 2016, accessed February 7, 2018, https://www.washingtonpost.com/news/the-fix/wp/2016/11/02/tracking-poll-finds-race-tied-as-trump-opens-up-an-8-point-edge-on-honesty/?utm_term=.3e25a38cca47.

19. George Washington, "The Rules of Civility," George Washington's Mount Vernon, http://www.mountvernon.org/george-washington/rules-of-civility/9/.

20. George Washington, "Washington's Inaugural Address (April 30, 1789)," National Archives, https://www.archives.gov/exhibits/american_originals/inaugtxt.html.

21. University of Pennsylvania, "Americans Know Surprisingly Little about Their Government, Survey Finds," The Annenberg Public Policy Center, last modified September 17, 2014, accessed February 10, 2018, https://www.annenbergpublicpolicycenter.org/wp-content/uploads/Civics-survey-press-release-09-17-2014-for-PR-Newswire.pdf.

22. "Just 37% of Americans Can Name Their Representative," Haven Insights, last modified May 31, 2017, accessed February 10, 2018, http://www.haveninsights.com/just-37-percent-name-representative/.

23. "Voting and Registration in the Election of November 2016," United States Census Bureau, last modified May 2017, accessed February 8, 2018, https://www.census.gov/data/tables/time-series/demo/voting-and-registration/p20-580.html.

24. Franklin Roosevelt, "State of the Union Message to Congress (January 11, 1944)," Franklin D. Roosevelt Presidential Library and Museum, accessed February 14, 2018, http://www.fdrlibrary.marist.edu/archives/address_text.html.

25. Isaiah Berlin, *Isaiah Berlin: Two Concepts of Liberty* (New York: Oxford University Press, 1969), 17, originally published 1969 as *Four Essays on Liberty*.

26. John Winthrop, "A Model of Christian Charity," Digital History, accessed March 3, 2018, http://www.digitalhistory.uh.edu/disp_textbook.cfm?smtID=3&psid=3918.

Bibliography

Abigail, Adams. "To Thomas Jefferson from Abigail Adams, with Enclosure, 6 June 1785." *Founders Online*. Accessed August 2, 2019. https://founders.archives.gov./?q=Recipient%3A%22Jefferson%2C%20Thomas%22%20Author%3A%22Adams%2C%20Abigail%22&s=1111311111&r=3.

Adams, John. "A Defense of the Constitutions of Government of the United States of America." Constitution Society. Accessed February 5, 2018. http://www.constitution.org/jadams/ja1_00.htm.

———. "From John Adams to Benjamin Rush, 4 April 1790." *Founders Online*. Last modified June 29, 2017. Accessed March 7, 2018. http://founders.archives.gov/documents/Adams/99-02-02-0903.

———. "From John Adams to John Rogers, 6 February 1801." *Founders Online*. Accessed September 10, 2016. http://founders.archives.gov/documents/Adams/99-02-02-4799.

———. "From John Adams to Massachusetts Militia, 11 October 1798." *Founders Online*. Accessed August 2, 2019. https://founders.archives.gov/documents/Adams/99-02-02-3102.

———. "John Adams Autobiography." Adams Family Papers. Accessed March 7, 2018. http://www.masshist.org/digitaladams/archive/doc?id=A1_35&bc=%2Fdigitaladams%2Farchive%2Fbrowse%2Fautobio1.php.

———. "John Adams to Zabdiel Adams, 21 June 1776." *Founders Online*. https://founders.archives.gov/documents/Adams/04-02-02-0011.

———. *John Adams: Writings from the New Nation 1784–1826*. Edited by Gordon S. Wood. New York: Library of America, 2011.

———. "Letter from John Adams to Abigail Adams (July 3, 1776)." Adams Family Papers. Accessed February 1, 2018. https://www.masshist.org/digitaladams/archive/doc?id=L17760703ja.

———. "Thoughts on Government (April 1776)." The Adams Papers Digital Editions. Accessed January 19, 2018. https://www.masshist.org/publications/apde2/view?&id=PJA04dg2.

———. "To Thomas Jefferson from John Adams." *Founders Online*. Accessed August 2, 2019. https://founders.archives.gov/documents/Jefferson/98-01-02-0977.

Adams, Samuel. "'Samuel Adams to James Warrern (1775).'" Samuel Adams Heritage Society. Last modified 2013. Accessed September 4, 2016. http://www.samuel-adams-heritage.com/documents/samuel-adams-to-james-warren-1775.html.

"The Address and Reasons of Dissent of the Minority of the Convention of Pennsylvania to Their Constituents (18 December 1787)." In *The Anti-Federalist: Writings by the Opponents of the Constitution*, edited by Herbert J. Storing and Murray Dry, 201–23. Nachdr. ed. Chicago: University of Chicago Press, 1985.

Agrippa. "Agrippa XII Part 1, To the Massachusetts Convention (January 11, 1788)." Teaching American History. Accessed January 28, 2018. http://teachingamericanhistory.org/library/document/agrippa-xii/.

———. "To the People (8 January 1788)." Letters of Agrippa. Accessed January 28, 2018. http://www.constitution.org/afp/agrippa.htm.

"Americans' Perceived Time Crunch No Worse Than in Past." Gallup. Last modified December 31, 2015. Accessed February 11, 2018. http://news.gallup.com/poll/187982/americans-perceived-time-crunch-no-worse-past.aspx.

"Americans' Worries about Most Crimes Similar to 2015." Gallup. Last modified November 14, 2016. Accessed February 11, 2018. http://Americans' Worries About Most Crimes Similar to 2015.

"Annapolis Convention. Address of the Annapolis Convention, [14 September 1786]." *Founders Online*. Accessed August 3, 2019. https://founders.archives.gov/documents/Hamilton/01-03-02-0556.

Arena, Valentina. "Roman sumptuary legislation: Three concepts of liberty." *European Journal of Political Theory* 10, no. 4 (2011): 463–89.

Bailyn, Bernard. *The Ideological Origins of the American Revolution*. Fiftieth anniversary edition. ed. Cambridge, MA: Belknap Press of Harvard University Press, 2017.

———. *To Begin the World Anew: The Genius and Ambiguities of the American Founders*. New York: Alfred A. Knopf, 2003.

Baker, Jennifer Jordan. "Benjamin Franklin's Autobiography and the Credibility of Personality." *Early American Literature* 35, no. 3 (2000): 274–93.

Becker, Carl. *The Declaration of Independence: A Study in the History of Political Ideas*. New York: Vintage Books, 1958.

Bellah, Robert Neelly, Richard Madsen, William M. Sullivan, Ann Swindler, and Steven M. Tipton. *Habits of the Heart: Individualism and Commitment in American Life*. Updated ed. Berkeley: University of California Press, 2008.

Bellezza, Silvia, Neeru Paharia, and Anat Keinan. "Research: Why Americans Are So Impressed by Busyness." *Harvard Business Review*. Last modified December 15, 2016. Accessed February 11, 2018. https://hbr.org/2016/12/research-why-americans-are-so-impressed-by-busyness.

Berlin, Isaiah. *Isaiah Berlin: Two Concepts of Liberty*. New York: Oxford University Press, 1969. Originally published 1969 as *Four Essays on Liberty*.

Bernstein, Richard B. *Thomas Jefferson*. Oxford [etc.]: Oxford University Press, 2005.

Boucher, Jonathan. "On Civil Liberty, Passive Obedience, and Nonresistance." Constitution Society. Accessed February 3, 2018. http://www.constitution.org/bcp/nonresis.htm.

Cappon, Lester J., ed. *The Adams-Jefferson Letters: The Complete Correspondence between Thomas Jefferson and Abigail and John Adams*. 1959 ed. Chapel Hill [u.a.]: University of North Carolina Press, 2001.

Carey, George. "Eighteenth Century: American Contributions." In *An Uncertain Legacy: Essays on the Pursuit of Liberty*, edited by Edward B. McLean, 112–33. Wilmington, DE: Intercollegiate Studies Institute, 1997.

Carey, George W., and James McClellan, eds. *The Federalist Papers: The Gideon Edition*. Gideon ed. Indianapolis: Liberty Fund, 2001.

Chernow, Ron. *Alexander Hamilton*. New York: Penguin Books, 2005.

Cicero, Marcus Tullius. *Cicero: On the Commonwealth and on the Laws*. Edited by James E. G Zetzel. Cambridge: Cambridge University Press, 1999.

———. *On Duties*. Edited by Miriam T. Griffin and E. M. Atkins. 23rd ed. Cambridge: Cambridge University Press, 2015.

Clement, Scott, and Emily Guskin. "Post-ABC Tracking Poll Finds Race Tied, as Trump Opens up an 8-Point Edge on Honesty." *Washington Post*. Last modified November 2, 2016. Accessed February 7, 2018. https://www.washingtonpost.com/news/the-fix/wp/2016/11/02/tracking-poll-finds-race-tied-as-trump-opens-up-an-8-point-edge-on-honesty/?utm_term=.3e25a38cca47.

Constant, Benjamin. "Benjamin Constant, from 'The Liberty of the Ancients Compared with the Liberty of the Moderns' (1819)." In *Freedom: A Philosophical Anthology*, edited by Ian Carter, Matthew H. Kramer, and Hillel Steiner, 15–20. Malden, MA: Blackwell Publishing, 2007.

———. "Benjamin Constant, the Liberty of Ancients Compared with that of Moderns (1819)." Online Library of Liberty: A Collection of Scholarly Works about Individual Liberty and Free Markets. Accessed February 12, 2019. https://oll.libertyfund.org/titles/constant-the-liberty-of-ancients-compared-with-that-of-moderns-1819.

Cooper, John M., and D. S. Hutchinson, eds. *Plato: Complete Works*. Indianapolis, IN: Hackett Publishing Company, 1997.
Corwin, Edward S. *John Marshall and the Constitution: A Chronicle of the Supreme Court*. Edited by Allen Johnson, Gerhard R. Lomer, and Charles W. Jefferys. Vol. 16. The Chronicles of America Series. New Haven: Yale University Press, 1919.
Cushman, Robert. "The Sin and Danger of Self-Love Described by a Sermon Preached at Plymouth, in New-England, 1621." Last modified October 30, 2013. Accessed August 12, 2015. http://www.gutenberg.org/files/44071/44071-h/44071-h.htm.
Dickinson, John. "The Letters of Fabius in 1788 on the Federal Constitution, Letter VIII." Edited by Paul L. Ford. Internet Archive. Accessed March 9, 2018. https://archive.org/stream/lettersoffabiusi00dickuoft/lettersoffabiusi00dickuoft_djvu.txt.
Engels, Jeremy. "Disciplining Jefferson: The Man within the Breast and the Rhetorical Norms of Producing Order." *Rhetoric & Public Affairs* 9, no. 3 (Fall 2006): 411–35.
Fears, J. Rufus. "Antiquity: The Example of Rome." In *An Uncertain Legacy: Essays on the Pursuit of Liberty*, edited by Edward B. McLean, 1–38. Wlmington, DE: Intercollegiate Studies Institute, 1997.
Fischer, David Hackett. *Liberty and Freedom*. Oxford: Oxford University Press, 2005.
Franklin, Benjamin. *Autobiography, Poor Richard, and Later Writings: Letters from London, 1757–1775, Paris, 1776–1785, Philadelphia, 1785–1790, Poor Richard's Almanack, 1733–1758, the Autobiography*. Edited by Joseph A. Leo Lemay. 5th ed. New York: Library of America, 2008.
———. "Benjamin Franklin, to the Abbes Chalut and Arnoux, April 1787." The Federalist Papers. Last modified December 2, 2012. Accessed February 4, 2020. https://thefederalistpapers.org/founders/franklin/benjamin-franklinto-the-abbes-chalut-and-arnoux-april-1787.
"'From Thomas Jefferson to John Taylor, 4 June 1798.' *Founders Online*. National Archives, version of January 18, 2019.'" Accessed January 27, 2019. https://founders.archives.gov/documents/Jefferson/01-30-02-0280.
Ganter, Herbert Lawrence. "Jefferson's 'Pursuit of Happiness' and Some Forgotten Men." *The William and Mary Quarterly*, 2nd ser., 16, no. 4 (October 1936).
"George Mason and Historic Human Rights Documents." Gunston Hall, Home of George Mason. Accessed March 7, 2018. http://gunstonhall.org/georgemason/rights.html.
Goss, Betty. "Public Speaking." Thomas Jefferson Encyclopedia. Last modified January 9, 2001. Accessed January 30, 2020. https://www.monticello.org/site/research-and-collections/public-speaking.
Hayek, Friedrich A. *The Constitution of Liberty: The Definitive Edition*. Edited by Ronald Hamowy. Chicago: University of Chicago Press, 2011.
Hechinger Report. "10 Most (and Least) Popular Advanced Placement (AP) Subjects." Education by the Numbers. Last modified February 12, 2014. Accessed March 28, 2019. http://educationbythenumbers.org/content/10-least-popular-advanced-placement-ap-subjects_930/
Herbert, Edward. "The Antient Religion of the Gentiles, and Causes of Their Errors Consider'd: the Mistakes and . . ." Translated by William Lewis. Internet Archive. Last modified January 15, 2008. Accessed January 21, 2020. https://archive.org/details/antientreligion00chergoog.
Hershman, James. "Jefferson's Head and Heart Letter." E-mail message to author. February 4, 2018.
Holmes, David Lynn. *The Religion of the Founding Fathers*. New York: Oxford University Press, 2006.
Holowchak, M. Andrew. "The 'Reluctant' Politician: Thomas Jefferson's Debt to Epicurus." *Eighteenth-Century Studies* 45, no. 2 (2012): 277–97.
Inwood, Brad, and Lloyd P. Gerson, trans. *The Epicurus Reader: Selected Writings and Testimonia*. Indianapolis: Hackett, 1994.
Jacobs, Jonathan A. *Aristotle's Virtues: Nature, Knowledge and Human Good*. New York: P. Lang, 2004.

Jefferson, Thomas. *Autobiography of Thomas Jefferson*. Mt. Pleasant, SC: Arcadia Press, 2017.

———. "Extract from Thomas Jefferson to St. John de Crèvecoeur (January 15, 1787)." Jefferson Quotes and Family Letters. Accessed March 4, 2018. http://tjrs.monticello.org/letter/8.

———. "From Thomas Jefferson to George Rogers Clark, 25 December 1780." *Founders Online*. https://founders.archives.gov/documents/Jefferson/01-04-02-0295.

———. "From Thomas Jefferson to Jedidiah Morse, 6 March 1822." *Founders Online*. National Archives. Last modified June 29, 2017. Accessed November 16, 2017. http://founders.archives.gov/documents/Jefferson/98-01-02-2700.

———. "From Thomas Jefferson to John Taylor, 4 June 1798." *Founders Online*. https://founders.archives.gov/documents/Jefferson/01-30-02-0280.

———. "From Thomas Jefferson to Maria Cosway, 12 October 1786." *Founders Online*. National Archives. Last modified June 29, 2017. Accessed November 8, 2017. https://founders.archives.gov/documents/Jefferson/01-10-02-0309.

———. "From Thomas Jefferson to Roger Chew Weightman, 24 June 1826." *Founders Online*. https://founders.archives.gov/?q=%20Author%3A%22Jefferson%2C%20Thomas%22%20Recipient%3A%22Weightman%2C%20Roger%20Chew%22&s=1111311111&r=1.

———. "Letter to George Rogers Clark, December 25, 1780." *Founders Online*. Accessed January 14, 2019. stps://founders.archives.gov/?q=jefferson%20empire%20of%20liberty%20Author%3A"Jefferson%2C%20Thomas"%20Recipient%3A"Clark%2C%20George%20Rogers"&s=1111311111&sa=&r=1&sr=clark.

———. "Letter to James Monroe, October 24, 1823." *Founders Online*. Accessed January 14, 2019. https://founders.archives.gov/?q=%20Author%3A%22Jefferson%2C%20Thomas%22%20Recipient%3A%22Monroe%2C%20James%22&s=1111311111&sa=&r=203&sr=.

———. "Notes on the Doctrine of Epicurus, [ca. 1799?]" *Founders Online*. Accessed September 10, 2016. http://founders.archives.gov/documents/Jefferson/01-31-02-0241.

———. *The Portable Thomas Jefferson*. Edited by Merrill D. Peterson. Harmondsworth: Penguin Books, 1985.

———. *The Portable Thomas Jefferson*. Edited by Merrill D. Peterson. Harmondsworth: Penguin Books, 1977.

———. "Query VIII. Population." Notes on the State of Virginia to *The Portable Thomas Jefferson*, edited by Merrill D. Peterson, 122–28. New York: Penguin Books, 1977.

———. "Thomas Jefferson to Benjamin Rush, 16 January 1811." *Founders Online*. Accessed August 2, 2019. https://founders.archives.gov/documents/Jefferson/03-03-02-0231.

———. "Thomas Jefferson to Charles Thomson, 9 January 1816." *Founders Online*. Accessed September 10, 2016. http://founders.archives.gov/documents/Jefferson/03-09-02-0216.

———. "Thomas Jefferson to Isaac McPherson, 13 August 1813." *Founders Online*. https://founders.archives.gov/documents/Jefferson/03-06-02-0322.

———. "Thomas Jefferson to William Stephens Smith, November 13, 1787." Jefferson Quotes and Family Letters. Accessed January 24, 2018. http://tjrs.monticello.org/letter/100.

———. "To James Madison from Thomas Jefferson, 30 August 1823." *Founders Online*. Last modified November 26, 2017. Accessed March 7, 2018. http://founders.archives.gov/documents/Madison/04-03-02-0113.

Jones, Howard Mumford. *The Pursuit of Happiness*. Cambridge: Harvard University Press, 1953.

"Just 37% of Americans can name their Representative." Haven Insights. Last modified May 31, 2017. Accessed February 10, 2018. http://www.haveninsights.com/just-37-percent-name-representative/.

Kant, Immanuel. *The Cambridge Edition of the Works of Immanuel Kant: Practical Philosophy*. Edited and translated by Mary J. Gregor. Cambridge: Cambridge University Press, 1996.
Kendall, Willmoore, and George W. Carey. *The Basic Symbols of the American Political Tradition*. Washington, DC: Catholic University of America Press, 1995. Digital file.
Lane, Melissa. "'Ancient Political Philosophy.'" Edited by Edward Zalta. The Stanford Encyclopedia of Philosophy (Summer 2017 Edition). URL = .
Lee, Richard Henry. "To George Washington from Richard Henry Lee, 11 October 1787." *Founders Online*. Last modified November 26, 2017. Accessed January 25, 2018. http://founders.archives.gov/documents/Washington/04-05-02-0336.
Lewis, C. S. *Mere Christianity: A Revised and Amplified Edition, with a New Introduction, of the Three Books Broadcast Talks, Christian Behaviour, and beyond Personality*. Fiftieth anniversary ed. London: HarperCollins Publishers, 2002.
Lienesch, Michael. "Historical Theory and Political Reform: Two Perspectives on Confederation Politics." *The Review of Politics* 45, no. 1 (January 1983): 94–115.
Liu, Dong, and Roy F. Baumeister. "Social Networking Online and Personality of Self-Worth: A Meta-Analysis." *Journal of Research and Personality* 64 (October 2016): 79–89.
Lochner v. New York, 198 S. Ct. (Apr. 17, 1906). Accessed August 3, 2019. https://supreme.justia.com/cases/federal/us/198/45/#tab-opinion-1921257.
Lochner v. New York, 198 Justia: US Supreme Court (Apr. 17, 1906). Accessed January 24, 2019. https://supreme.justia.com/cases/federal/us/198/45/#tab-opinion-1921257.
Locke, John. *Second Treatise of Government*. Edited by C. B. MacPherson. Indianapolis: Hackett Publishing, 1980.
Lutz, Donald S. *The Origins of American Constitutionalism*. Baton Rouge: Louisiana State University Press, 1988.
———. *A Preface to American Political Theory*. Lawrence: University Press of Kansas, 1992.
Madison, James. "From James Madison to Thomas Jefferson, 19 March 1787." *Founders Online*. Last modified November 26, 2017. Accessed January 25, 2018. https://founders.archives.gov/documents/Madison/01-09-02-0169.
———. *James Madison: Writings*. Edited by Jack N. Rakove. New York: Literary Classics of the United States, 2011.
———. "Special Message to Congress on the Foreign Policy Crisis—War Message." Speech, June 1, 1812. Presidential Speeches: James Madison Presidency. https://millercenter.org/the-presidency/presidential-speeches/june-1-1812-special-message-congress-foreign-policy-crisis-war.
———. "Speech to the Virginia Ratifying Convention, June 6, 1788." Constitution Society. Accessed August 3, 2019. http://www.constitution.org/rc/rat_va_05.htm.
———. "Vices of the Political System of the United States (1787)." National Humanities Center. Accessed August 15, 2015. http://americainclass.org/sources/makingrevolution/constitution/text1/madisonvices.pdf.
"Majority in U.S. No Longer Thinks Trump Keeps His Promises." Gallup. Last modified April 17, 2017. Accessed February 7, 2018. http://news.gallup.com/poll/208640/majority-no-longer-thinks-trump-keeps-promises.aspx.
Malone, Dumas. *Jefferson the Virginian*. Vol. 1 of *Jefferson and His Time*. Boston: Little, Brown and Company, 1948.
Massachusetts Historical Society. "The Votes and Proceedings of the Freeholders and other Inhabitants of the Town of Boston, in Town Meeting Assembled." Coming of the American Revolution. Accessed January 11, 2018. https://www.masshist.org/database/viewer.php?item_id=609.
"Mayflower Compact, 1620." The Avalon Project: Documents in Law, History, and Diplomacy. https://founders.archives.gov/documents/Adams/04-02-02-0011.
McClure, Christopher S. "Learning from Franklin's Mistakes: Self-Interest Rightly Understood in the Autobiography." *The Review of Politics* 76 (2014): 69–92.

Miles, Richard D. "The American Image of Benjamin Franklin." *American Quarterly* 9, no. 2 (Summer 1957): 117–43.
Montesquieu, Charles Louis de Secondat de. *The Spirit of the Laws*. Edited by Anne M. Cohler, Basia C. Miller, and Harold S. Stone. Cambridge: Cambridge University Press, 2009.
Monticello. "Maria Cosway (Engraving)." Research and Collections. Accessed February 4, 2018. https://www.monticello.org/site/research-and-collections/maria-cosway-engraving.
Mulford, Carla. "Figuring Benjamin Franklin in American Cultural Memory." *The New England Quarterly* 72, no. 3 (1999).
Mulgan, Richard. "Liberty in Ancient Greece." In *Conceptions of Liberty in Political Philosophy*, edited by Zbigniew Pelczynski and John Gray, 7–26. London: Athlone Press, 1984.
My Fellow Americans: Presidential Inaugural Addresses, from George Washington to Barack Obama. St. Petersburg, FL: Red and Black Publishers, 2009.
National Archives. "Annapolis Convention. Address of the Annapolis Convention, (14 September 1786)." Founders Online. Accessed March 9, 2018. https://founders.archives.gov/documents/Hamilton/01-03-02-0556.
"New Hampshire Constitution (1776)." The Avalon Project: Documents in Law, History, and Diplomacy. Accessed March 8, 2018. http://avalon.law.yale.edu/18th_century/nh09.asp.
Novak, Michael. *On Two Wings: Humble Faith and Common Sense at the American Founding*. San Francisco, CA: Encounter Books, 2002.
Paine, Thomas. *Common Sense*. Philadelphia, 1776. Reprint. New York: Fall River Press, 1995.
Pangle, Thomas L. "Republicanism and Rights." In *The Framers and Fundamental Rights*, edited by Robert A. Licht, 102–20. Washington, DC: AEI Press, 1991.
———. *The Spirit of Modern Republicanism: The Moral Vision of the American Founders and the Philosophy of Locke*. Chicago: University of Chicago Press, 1990.
Pestana, Carla Gardina, and Sharon V. Salinger, eds. *Inequality in Early America*. Hanover, NH: University Press of New England, 1999.
Peterson, Merrill D., ed. *The Portable Thomas Jefferson*. Harmondsworth, Eng.: Penguin Books, 1977.
———. *Thomas Jefferson and the New Nation: A Biography*. New York: Oxford University Press, 1970.
Plato. *Plato Complete Works*. Edited by John M. Cooper and D. S. Hutchinson. Translated by G. M. A. Grube and C. D. C Reeve. Indianapolis, IN: Hackett Publishing Company, 1997.
Plutarch. "Solon." In *Plutarch's Lives*, edited by Arthur Hugh Clough. Vol. I. New York: The Modern Library, 2001.
"Political Splits Widen on Satisfaction With Life in U.S." Gallup. Last modified January 25, 2018. Accessed February 6, 2018. http://news.gallup.com/poll/226211/political-splits-widen-satisfaction-life.aspx?g_source=CATEGORY_WELLBEING&g_medium=topic&g_campaign=tiles.
Putnam, Robert D. *Bowling Alone: The Collapse and Revival of American Community*. Nachdr. ed. New York: Simon & Schuster, 2007.
Raaflaub, Kurt. *The Discovery of Freedom in Ancient Greece*. Translated by Renate Franciscono. Chicago: University of Chicago Press, 2004.
"Research & Collections: Isaac H. Tiffany." Thomas Jefferson Monticello. https://www.monticello.org/site/research-and-collections/isaac-h-tiffany.
Richard, Carl J. *The Founders and the Classics: Greece, Rome and the American Enlightenment*. Cambridge, MA: Harvard Univeristy Press, 1996.
———. *Greeks and Romans Bearing Gifts: How the Ancients Inspired the Founding Fathers*. Lanham, Md.: Rowman & Littlefield Publishers, 2008.

Roosevelt, Franklin. "State of the Union Message to Congress (January 11, 1944)." Franklin D. Roosevelt Presidential Library and Museum. Accessed February 14, 2018. http://www.fdrlibrary.marist.edu/archives/address_text.html.

Sandel, Michael J. *Democracy's Discontent: America in Search of a Public Philosophy*. Cambridge, MA: Belknap Press of Harvard University Press, 1996.

Schmidtz, David, and Jason Brennan. *A Brief History of Liberty*. Chichester, UK: Wiley-Blackwell, 2010.

Schofield, Malcolm. "Aristotle's Political Ethics." In *The Blackwell Guide to Aristotle's Nicomachean Ethics*, edited by Richard Kraut, 305–22. Malden, MA: Blackwell Publishing, 2006.

Shain, Barry Alan. *The Myth of American Individualism: The Protestant Origins of American Political Thought*. Princeton, NJ: Princeton University Press, 1994.

Sheldon, Garrett Ward. "The Political Theory of the Declaration of Independence." 2002. In *The Declaration of Independence: Origins and Impact*, edited by Scott Douglas Gerber, 16–28. Washington, DC: CQ Press, 2002.

Shimer, David. "Yale's Most Popular Class Ever: Happiness." *New York Times*, January 26, 2018. https://www.nytimes.com/2018/01/26/nyregion/at-yale-class-on-happiness-draws-huge-crowd-laurie-santos.html.

Skinner, Quentin. *Liberty before Liberalism*. Cambridge: Cambridge University Press, 1998.

Soni, Vivasvan. *Mourning Happiness: Narrative and the Politics of Modernity*. Ithaca, NY: Cornell University Press, 2010.

St. John De Crevecoeur, J. Hector. "Letters from an American Farmer." American Studies Virtual Classrooms @ UVA. Accessed August 14, 2015. http://xroads.virginia.edu/~HYPER/CREV/header.html.

Storing, Herbert J., and Murray Dry, eds. *The Anti-Federalist: Writings by the Opponents of the Constitution*. Nachdr. ed. Chicago: University of Chicago Press, 1985.

Thucydides. "Pericles' Funeral Oration." University of Minnesota Human Rights Library. Accessed January 5, 2018. http://hrlibrary.umn.edu/education/thucydides.html.

Tocqueville, Alexis de. *Democracy in America*. Translated by James T. Schleifer. Edited by Eduardo Nolla. English ed. Vol. 1. Indianapolis: Liberty Fund, 2012.

———. *The Old Regime and the Revolution*. Translated by John Bonner. New York: Harper and Brothers, 1856. Accessed February 9, 2018. http://oll.libertyfund.org/titles/2419.

Tufts, Joshua. "The Believers Most Sure Freedom Purchased by Jesus Christ, Laid Down in a Sermon Preached at Narragansett, No 1. 1757. By Joshua Tufts, A.M. Preacher of the Gospel There. Published at the Desire of the Hearers." Early American Imprints. Accessed February 2, 2018. http://0-infoweb.newsbank.com.gull.georgetown.edu/iw-search/we/Evans?p_theme=eai&p_product=EAIX&d_collections=EVAN&d_collectionName=EVAN&p_action=doc&p_topdoc=1&p_docnum=1&d_searchform=customized&p_text_custbase-0=8051&p_field_custbase-0=docnum&p_sort=YMD_date:D&p_nbid=M43U43WAMTUxNzU5NDczMy4yNDQwNzg6MToxMzoxNDEuMTYxLjM4LjQ1&p_docref=.

Tully, James. "Locke on Liberty." In *Conceptions of Liberty in Political Philosophy*, edited by Zbigniew Pelczynski and John Gray, 57–82. London: Athlone Press, 1984.

Turkle, Sherry. *Alone Together: Why We Expect More from Technology and Less from Each Other*. New York: Basic Books, 2001.

University of Pennsylvania. "Americans Know Surprisingly Little about Their Government, Survey Finds." The Annenberg Public Policy Center. Last modified September 17, 2014. Accessed February 10, 2018. https://www.annenbergpublicpolicycenter.org/wp-content/uploads/Civics-survey-press-release-09-17-2014-for-PR-Newswire.pdf.

"Virginia Declaration of Rights." The Avalon Project: Documents in Law, History, and Diplomacy. Accessed March 7, 2018. http://avalon.law.yale.edu/18th_century/virginia.asp.

"Voting and Registration in the Election of November 2016." United States Census Bureau. Last modified May 2017. Accessed February 8, 2018. https://www.census.gov/data/tables/time-series/demo/voting-and-registration/p20-580.html.

Washington, George. "The Rules of Civility." George Washington's Mount Vernon. http://www.mountvernon.org/george-washington/rules-of-civility/9/.

———. "Washington's Inaugural Address (April 30, 1789)." National Archives. https://www.archives.gov/exhibits/american_originals/inaugtxt.html.

Weaver, David R. "Leadership, Locke, and the Federalist." *American Journal of Political Science* 41, no. 2 (April 1997): 420–46.

Weinberger, Jerry. *Benjamin Franklin Unmasked: On the Unity of His Moral, Religious, and Political Thought*. Lawrence: University Press of Kansas, 2005.

"What Next? Harper's Weekly, April 22, 1865, (Editorial)." Harpweek. Accessed March 9, 2018. http://education.harpweek.com/TheReconstructionConvention/TheBeliefs/Belief7/Belief7-r003.htm.

Williams, Walter E., ed. "What the Founders Said About Slavery." Quotations from Framers of the Constitution and Others. Last modified July 2, 2015. Accessed February 7, 2018. http://econfaculty.gmu.edu/wew/quotes/slavery.html.

Wills, Garry. *Inventing America: Jefferson's Declaration of Independence*. Garden City, NY: Doubleday & Company, 1978.

———. *James Madison*. New York: Times Books, 2002.

Winthrop, John. "A Model of Christian Charity." Digital History. Accessed March 3, 2018. http://www.digitalhistory.uh.edu/disp_textbook.cfm?smtID=3&psid=3918.

———. "On Liberty (1645)." Constitution Society. Accessed February 3, 2018. http://www.constitution.org/bcp/winthlib.htm.

Wood, Gordon S. *The Americanization of Benjamin Franklin*. New York: Penguin Press, 2005.

———. *The Creation of the American Republic: 1776–1787*. Chapel Hill: University of North Carolina Press, 1998.

———. *Revolutionary Characters: What Made the Founders Different*. New York: Penguin Books, 2007.

Yakobson, A. "TRADITIONAL POLITICAL CULTURE AND THE PEOPLE'S ROLE IN THE ROMAN REPUBLIC." *Historia: Zeitschrift Für Alte Geschichte* 59, no. 3 (2010): 282–302. Accessed January 9, 2018. http://proxy.library.georgetown.edu/login?url=https://search.proquest.com/docview/746422617?accountid=11091.

Yarbrough, Jean M. *American Virtues: Thomas Jefferson on the Character of a Free People*. Lawrence: University Press of Kansas, 1998.

Yates, Robert. "Notes of the Secret Debates of the Federal Convention of 1787, Taken by the Late Hon Robert Yates, Chief Justice of the State of New York, and One of the Delegates from That State to the Said Convention." The Avalon Project: Documents in Law, History, and Poltitics. Accessed January 28, 2018. http://avalon.law.yale.edu/18th_century/yates.asp.

Young, Mark A. *Negotiating the Good Life: Aristotle and the Civil Society*. Aldershot: Ashgate, 2005.

Index

Adams, John: Benjamin Franklin's reputation, 54; democracy, 31; letter to Abigail, x, 92; moral superiority of Americans, 2, 3; virtuous citizens, 74
Annapolis Convention, 78
antifederalists : beliefs, 70, 85–86, 87, 107; Federalists alarming fears, 76, 84
Aristotle, 21–25; friendship, 25; happiness, 15; ultimate human function, 23; virtue, 24, 109
Articles of Confederation, 71, 74–75

Bailyn, Bernard, xiv
Bellah, Robert: American values, 108; *Habits of the Heart*, 107
Berlin, Isaiah: meaning of freedom, 3, 112; negative and positive liberty, 4
Boucher, Jonathan, 42–43
busyness, 109

Calhoun, John C., xi
Carey, George, xviii
Christianity, 40–43; American political movements impact on, 40
Cicero, 1, 26–28
Cincinnatus, 90
Civil War, 96–103
Clinton, Hilary, 110
Constant, Benjamin, 5
Constitution. *See* United States Constitution
critical period, 69, 71, 75, 77
Cushman, Robert, 41

de Crevecoeur, Hector St. Jean, 97
de Tocqueville, Alexis: administrative centralization, 97, 98, 102; American tour, 96; box with a false bottom, 96, 111; equality, 97; federalism advantages of, 100–101; individualism, 97, 99; industrialization, 99; mores, 100; presidency, 101–102
Declaration of Independence, 9, 11
Deism, 43–44
Democracy in America, 96
democracy, 31

eleutheria, 32–34
Epicurus, 25–26
eudaimonia, 22

The Federalist Papers: No. 10, 89; No. 51, 89; No.55, 90
federalists: national government strengthened, 83; virtuous leadership, 88, 89, 90–91
Franklin, Benjamin: *Autobiography*, 52–53, 55–60; childhood and young life, 55–56; *A Dissertation on Liberty & Necessity, Pleasure and Pain*, 57; errata, 56–57; virtues, 58–59; virtuous citizens, 83
freedom, origin of the word, 4

Hamilton, Alexander: science of politics, 77–78; vigorous government, 88
happiness: colonial interest in, xiii; Constitution absent from, 71–74; Declaration, 10–12; origin of the word, 22; revolutionary writings, 12–13
Henry, Patrick: critic of Constitution, x, 84; critical of federalists, 84

immigration, fear of, xi

Jefferson, Thomas: advice to his nephew, 19; Declaration, influences on, 14; immigrants, xi; last letter, ix; Maria Cosway letter, 51, 60–64; Monroe Doctrine, xi; opinion of Greek government, 31–32; three greatest men, 44

Lee, Richard Henry, 10
liberatas, 35–36
liberty, origin of the word, 4
Locke, John, 44, 47; Declaration of Independence influence on, 40, 45; natural law, 45

Madison, James: language limitations of, 3; Confederation Congress problems with, 75–76, 87
Mayflower Compact, 41–42
moderation central to the good life, 2
Montesquieu, 86–87, 95

Nicomachean Ethics, 22

Paine, Thomas, x
Pangle, Thomas, xvi

Pericles' Funeral Oration, xvii, 33
public good liberty, 3
Puritans, 41
Putnam, Robert : *Bowling Alone* , 107, 108–109

Roosevelt, Franklin, 111–112

Shays' Rebellion, 75
slavery, connection to freedom, 33, 35, 42
social media, impact of, 96
Solon, 32

Trump, Donald, 110

United States Constitution, 78; ratification, 79, 92

Washington, George: first inaugural address, xviii, 110; *110 Rules of Civility*, 110
Webster, Daniel, xi
Winthrop, James, 86
Winthrop, John, 41, 42, 112

About the Author

Heather Dutton Dudley graduated summa cum laude from the University of Maryland, and holds a master's degree in history from George Mason University, a master's degree in psychology from American University, and a doctorate in liberal studies from Georgetown University. Teaching and studying have always been both her vocation and avocation. She has taught at the high school and college levels, and especially loves teaching courses for senior citizens on the Declaration of Independence and the US Constitution. She is a former competitive runner and competes in the equestrian sport of dressage. She has two sons, many grandchildren, and lives with her husband in Upperville, Virginia.